REMEMBERING

SUMMERFIELD

Glimpses of the Past

GLADYS H. SCARLETTE

THE History PRESS

Published by The History Press
Charleston, SC 29403
www.historypress.net

First published 2009

Front cover, top to bottom: John H. Barker store. *Courtesy Summerfield Town Hall Museum*; Yance Waynick and Richard "Dick" Hoskins with mules, about 1935. *The Hoskins Collection, courtesy Greensboro Historical Museum*.
Back cover, top to bottom: Gray Gables. *Courtesy Bill Gordon*; Summerfield Town Hall, formerly the Brittain Store. *Courtesy the author*; Summerfield Town Seal. *Courtesy Town of Summerfield*; Ready for an Easter egg hunt, about 1953, at the home of Mr. and Mrs. W.A. Scarlette, Grandma and Pa to the children. *Courtesy the author*.

Manufactured in the United States

ISBN 978.1.59629.783.8

Library of Congress CIP data applied for.

Contents

ACKNOWLEDGEMENTS

I'd like to thank all who had a part in making this book possible, especially those who were willing to share their memories.

For her help and advice, I want to thank Mary Browning.

I'm grateful for those reporters in the past and their information about everyday events in our little community. They might seem unimportant to many, but without their stories we would have missed out on some interesting tidbits of our history.

Many thanks to the Greensboro Public Library for the use of its microfilmed copies of old newspapers, especially the *Greensboro Patriot*, the *Greensboro Daily News* and the *Greensboro Record*. Much of the information for this book was found in those papers.

I hope future generations will appreciate these glimpses into our past.

Introduction

Summerfield, North Carolina, was originally known as Bruce's Crossroads, in honor of Charles Bruce, one of the earliest and most prominent landowners. The name was changed to Summerfield by 1812 when the first post office was established, with Charles Bruce as the first postmaster.

There is some confusion regarding the name of the village. According to tradition, Reverend John Summerfield came to the village to preach, and the town was named for him. No records have been found to substantiate the tradition. However, an obituary for Charles Bruce from the *Tarboro Free Press* of Tarboro, North Carolina, dated March 20, 1832, states:

> *Died at the house of his son-in-law, Maj. Abraham Peoples, in Guilford Co., NC on Jan. 21st last, Charles Bruce, Esq., aged 90 years and 10 days. Mr. Bruce was a native of Westmoreland Co., Va., whence he emigrated to North Carolina, and in the year 1769 settled in Guilford Co., NC at a place which he called Summerfield, where he has resided ever since. He was a member of the Convention that formed the State Constitution in 1776, for several years, about the close of the Revolutionary War, was a member of the State legislature, and was for the last thirty years, a member of the Baptist church.*

Hillsdale Primitive Baptist Church; part of the building is original. *Courtesy Irene Clodfelter.*

It seems likely that Charles Bruce was a member of what is now Hillsdale Primitive Baptist Church located on Scalesville Road. It appears to be the oldest church in the Summerfield area. The deed dated June 12, 1784, mentions the "Haw River Meetinghouse," "the benefits of the spring for the congregation" and "the Society of people called Regular Baptists." Evidently, the church was there before June 1784. Charles Bruce was appointed to contract for a box to hold the church book and papers; no date was given for the entry, but the next entry was dated April 7, 1822.

Other churches in the area came later: Summerfield Baptist Church, now First Baptist, was organized in 1860. According to "Miss Kate" Hoskins, John and Lydia Hoskins built a church on their own land and allowed anyone to use it for religious purposes. Miss Kate stated that the Northern Methodist Church eventually bought the building and gave it to the local African Americans. The church is now named Peace United Methodist Church. The Summerfield United Methodist Church was established in 1888 according to Ethel Trogdon's book *The History of the Summerfield United Methodist Church.* Many other churches were established in later years.

During the Revolutionary War, "Lighthorse Harry" Lee's bugler, James Gillies, was killed by British soldiers near Summerfield. Gillies was just a young lad and was unarmed at the time of his death. His story so endeared him to the people of Summerfield that a bugle appears on the town seal. The first school newspaper was named the *Bugler*, and the first school annual, or yearbook, was called *Bugle Notes*.

Education was, and is, important to the people of Summerfield. The earliest record of a school found is the log school, which was located on Oak Ridge Road. One of the teachers there was the grandfather of O'Henry, the famous writer. He and Nathaniel Boyden, who later became a North Carolina Supreme Court justice, were headed to South Carolina and Georgia when their stagecoach stopped for the night at Summerfield. The innkeeper, Hezekiah Saunders, told them of the need for teachers, and William Sydney Porter decided to teach at Summerfield for part of a year while Boyden taught nearby at King's Crossroads.

Later, the small village was home to two academies, Blair Academy, or Summerfield High School, and later the Summerfield Academy and Business Institute. One of the earliest rural high schools was built in Summerfield in 1911 with a lot of help from the community. Students from other areas with no high school came to Summerfield and boarded with local families. The old log school was used as a dormitory for boys attending the high school.

The smokehouse, built during the Civil War era according to Margaret Metz, is located in the historic district. *Courtesy the author.*

Above: The Charles H. Willson House was built about 1858 by Willson, a farmer and merchant. *Courtesy Terry Spencer and Linda Southard.*

Below: Gray Gables, a beautiful Victorian house, was built by Henry Clay Brittain in 1903. *Courtesy Bill Gordon.*

The first passenger train to Summerfield arrived on July 31, 1886. The coming of the railroad caused a small building boom in Summerfield; by 1887, it was reported that two new stores and sixteen new dwellings had been built. The last passenger train through Summerfield was April 30, 1939, but freight service continued for a number of years.

For many years, the majority of Summerfield residents were farmers, but now most of the farms have become housing developments. A few barns, tobacco barns and other remnants of farm buildings remain in the area. A smokehouse built in the 1800s is still standing in the historic district.

Many of the houses located in the historic district were built by local merchants. Among them are the R.V. Harris House, the Charles Willson House, the John Medearis House, the N.W. Ogburn House and the H.C. Brittain House, which was called Gray Gables. An even older house at the crossroads was said to have been built by Alexander Strong Martin.

The old G.J. Smith brick store, which was later R.C. Gordon Hardware Store, a frame store built by R.V. Harris, and Charles H. Willson's store, no longer standing, were located at the crossroads. The H.C. Brittain store,

Alexander Strong Martin is believed to have built this house about 1835. He was the natural son of Governor Alexander Martin. *Courtesy Bill Gordon.*

Above: Completed in 1896, the Noah Webster Ogburn House is shown here during the 1920s. *Courtesy Elizabeth Hoskins.*

Below: Saunders Inn, built about 1822, was the local stagecoach stop. *Courtesy North Carolina Collection, University of North Carolina Library at Chapel Hill.*

The store built by George J. Smith about 1877, according to his granddaughter, Margaret Metz. When this photograph was made about 1950, it was Gordon Hardware Store. *Courtesy Bill Gordon.*

Above: This frame store was built by R.V. Harris before 1900 and has been operated by various people. The store has been vacant for many years. *Courtesy the author.*

Below: A view inside Charles H. Willson's store, in the early 1900s, with Mr. Willson and the delivery boy. *Courtesy Betsy Willson Greeson.*

Truman and Judy Doggett's truck in the 2009 Founder's Day Parade. *Courtesy the author.*

now the town hall, is also located at the crossroads. Although the Saunders Inn, built about 1822 by Hezekiah Saunders, is not located in the historic district, it is of historic interest.

Summerfield was incorporated in 1996, and the first mayor was Bill Peterson; the present mayor is Mark Brown. Over the years, the town has grown from a handful of farmers to over seven thousand residents. One of the latest improvements to the town is the Summerfield Park, located near the elementary school. There is a large lake available for fishing, along with picnic tables, walking trails and a playground for children. An amphitheatre, outdoor classroom, fitness equipment, paved trails and an additional playground and restroom have recently been completed. A fishing pier, picnic shelter and rain garden have also been added. Work has begun on a town ball field that will have space for the Recreation League teams to play softball, soccer and other sports.

The first Founders Day was held in 1996 and has been observed each year since. One of the highlights of the day is the parade. With over two hundred entries, there are old automobiles, fire trucks and floats from businesses, churches and civic groups. Many politicians and would-be politicians also take part in the parade. The children look forward to the candy and other items given out by most of the parade entrants. Summerfield Town Hall, formerly Brittain's Store, is located at the original Bruce's Crossroads in the historic district. The town hall contains a small museum with historic items related to Summerfield history and is open to the public Monday through Friday from 8:30 a.m. until 4:30 p.m. except for holidays. Visitors are welcome.

PART I

People

THE "PAUL REVERE" OF BRUCE'S CROSSROADS

Much has been written about Charles Bruce and James Gillies, the bugle boy, in connection with "Lighthorse Harry" Lee at the beginning of the Revolution. But what about Isaac Wright, the man who risked his life to warn of the approach of the British troops? On the morning of February 12, 1781, while out on his pony, Wright spotted the British. He probably had heard that "Lighthorse Harry" and his men were in the neighborhood, so off he went to warn them.

Lee and his troops were about to eat a late breakfast about noon at Bruce's home when Wright rode up and told them he had spotted some British dragoons two or three miles up the road. Lee sent Captain Armstrong with a small detachment to verify the report and insisted that Wright go along. Since Wright's pony was already tired, he was given the fine horse that Gillies, the bugler, rode. Gillies, worried about his horse, jumped on Wright's pony and hurried off after the men.

When they had traveled two or three miles and hadn't spotted the British, Armstrong accused Wright of making a false report. Wright assured him that he had seen the British but that he might have been wrong about the distance. Two of the soldiers and Gillies agreed to go farther and soon found proof of Wright's story.

A squad of British dragoons, led by Captain Miller, had stopped by the side of the road and couldn't be seen until Wright and the others were almost upon them. There was nothing they could do but try to outrun the dragoons.

With the British hot on their trail, the bugle boy on Wright's tired pony didn't stand a chance. When he was overtaken by the British, they showed him no mercy and cut him to pieces. This happened near the home of the Reverend Henry Tatum.

When Armstrong and his detachment came upon the scene, Colonel Banastre Tarleton and his corps charged toward them at full speed. Armstrong had no choice but to retreat. Meanwhile, Lee, apparently anticipating more trouble, waited with the rest of his men near the road, where they couldn't be seen.

When Armstrong came by, pursued by Tarleton and his corps, Lee intercepted them and fought so fiercely that a large number were killed. Lee, upset upon hearing of Gillies' death, held Miller responsible and would have hung him on the spot but, because of the fighting, Lee sent him off to General Greene as a prisoner of war.

Lee's legion headed for Virginia, and the British troops spent the night at the Bruce home. The next morning they left it in a pitiable condition. They burned fences and outbuildings, took all the grain and other provisions and were ready to set fire to the house when John and Richard Robinson, two Quakers who lived nearby, arrived and persuaded the British to leave it be.

In the Reverend Eli W. Caruthers's account of the skirmish at Bruce's Crossroads, Wright is referred to as a countryman. In 1779, he acquired 1,072 acres, in 1780 he acquired 1,050 acres and he added more acreage in later years. When the 1790 census was taken, Wright was listed in Guilford County along with his wife, four sons, three daughters and seven slaves. In the same census, Bruce was listed as the owner of ten slaves.

Sometime after 1798, Wright moved to Rutherford County, Tennessee, where he owned a gristmill, a sawmill and a cotton machine, as well as a large farm. Would the cotton machine have been a cotton gin? If so, Wright was well aware of what was going on in the world about him. Eli Whitney had just invented the cotton gin in 1793. In his will, dated February 7, 1812, he mentions more than nine hundred acres and seven slaves. One interesting thing about the slaves mentioned in the will was the Negro man Sam. Wright specified that "if Sam should wish his freedom at my death he may have it being hired out until he pays one hundred and fifty dollars, but if not he may continue to be my wife's property her life time." Some of Wright's children lived in Tennessee, but his son Isaac Jr. lived in Randolph County, North Carolina. When his wife, Rebekah, died, she left all of her property to her daughters. She specified that none of her sons or their children was to receive any part of her estate. Had women's lib already started in Tennessee?

Sometimes You Win, Sometimes You Lose

Jesse Hoskins, sometimes referred to as the Earl of Summerfield, had a passion for politics. During the Republican Convention in 1886, he was so sure that the Democrats would win that he pledged to "take off his shoes and stockings and hoof it barefooted from Currituck to Cherokee" if North Carolina and Guilford County went Republican.

He got lucky and didn't have to take that long walk. It was probably a good thing because he apparently suffered from rheumatism. In 1889, he traveled to Hot Springs, Arkansas, for treatment. The springs seemed to be just what Hoskins needed, and he improved rapidly. During the same year, Hoskins also went to Washington for the inauguration.

Several years later, James W. Friddle of Stokesdale wasn't so lucky. Positive that the Patriots baseball team would win the Carolina Association pennant in 1911, he wagered with E.B. Moore, who bet on Winston's Twins. If the Patriots lost, Mr. Friddle agreed to roll a wheelbarrow from Stokesdale to Greensboro, a distance of about eighteen miles. If the Twins lost, Moore agreed to roll a wheelbarrow to Winston-Salem. There must have been two very anxious fans at those ball games.

When Mr. Friddle realized that he had lost the bet, he started making preparations to keep his promise. On a Saturday afternoon in September, he rolled his wheelbarrow about seven miles from Stokesdale and left it in a buggy, returning back home to spend Sunday with his family.

On Monday morning at 3:00 a.m., he left home and returned to his wheelbarrow. According to the wager, he was to arrive in Greensboro at ten o'clock in the morning. He started pushing the barrow again and rolled it into Greensboro only two minutes behind schedule.

A large crowd had gathered at the courthouse square to meet Mr. Friddle as he proudly rolled his dilapidated wheelbarrow up Elm

Street. Bystanders applauded as he passed Market Street and rolled the wheelbarrow into the entrance of King's Cigar Store, where he received congratulations from his Greensboro friends for his pluck in standing by the Greensboro team. His enthusiastic fans presented him with a box of fine cigars to show their appreciation.

Mr. Friddle mopped his brow and declared that the weather was warm. No one doubted the sincerity of his remark since he had pushed the wheelbarrow about eleven miles. He was still smiling and making the best of the situation as he went down the street. One of the fans urged him to make the same wager again the next year and make Mr. Moore do some pushing. Mr. Friddle declined. He laughed and said that he was afraid to make any more bets.

Please Pass the Mud Pie

When I was growing up in Summerfield, we didn't have TVs, CDs, DVDs, iPods and all the other modern technology. We had dolls and a few store-bought toys, but we did most of our playing outside.

Before we could play, we had to get our work done. We drew buckets of water from the well and carried armloads of wood for the cookstove. When it came time for a wheat threshing or corn shucking, it seemed like hundreds of gallons of water and truckloads of wood were needed for cooking enough for all the folks who came to help with the harvesting.

But the work was worth it when we got to eat all that good food. Mama and my oldest sister made rice pudding, in big dishpans, and all kinds of pies, besides the meat and vegetables. We raised most of the food on the farm and had a cow for milk and butter—and all the whipped cream you could want.

We even made play out of some of our work. When Daddy and the boys sawed and split wood for the cookstove, we stacked it up so that it would dry out—two sticks turned one way and two sticks turned the other way, about six or eight stacks high. We called them pigpens.

In the summer, we worked in tobacco, dropping small plants one at a time into a tobacco planter up and down the rows until the whole field was planted. Those rows seemed awfully long. When the tobacco grew bigger, we had to pull the suckers from each plant; the suckers grew on the stalk at the end of each leaf. That wasn't as bad as pulling off the tobacco worms and stepping on them to kill them. Ugh! What a messy job.

When it came time to pull the tobacco leaves for curing, the women and children worked at the tobacco barn stringing the tobacco. The children usually handed the leaves to a stringer, who tied the leaves onto the sticks, which were then hung in the tobacco barn and cured with wood fires. Sometimes we'd go to the watermelon patch, cut several watermelons, slice them with tobacco twine and eat them without washing the tobacco gum off our hands. Lots of days, one of the children would go to the house and bring back butter and jelly biscuits for all of us.

We made playhouses by stringing old tobacco twine around small trees. We marked off the rooms that way. We made plenty of mud pies and cakes. When the men chopped down trees and left big chips of wood, we used them for our bread to make pretend sandwiches, and the "beans" from redbud trees became our beans.

We used grapevines in the woods to swing on, but we had a real swing in the yard made from a plank and a rope tied to a limb. We never had a swing made from a tire.

When we visited our cousins, we played all kinds of games: Mother, may I?; giant step; snake in the gully; bum bum bum; drop the handkerchief; spin the bottle; rock school; and probably others that I've forgotten. After a rain, when the sand or dirt was just the right consistency, we'd put our bare foot down and pat sand on top of it. Then we'd very carefully slip our foot out, and if you did it right, it wouldn't cave in. We called them toad frog houses. Sometimes they didn't last long because somebody would come along and smash them in.

One of our favorite jump rope rhymes was: "Mama, Mama, I feel sick; Send for the doctor quick, quick quick; Doctor, Doctor, shall I die? Yes, my child, but do not cry…How many cars will be at my funeral?" Then you jumped until you missed, and the number you missed on would be the number of cars at your funeral! Sounds a little morbid, but we didn't think so then.

On rainy days, we got out the paper dolls. We had a few store-bought ones, but we also cut out paper dolls from old pattern books and had just as much fun with them. We made furniture for our paper dolls from cardboard and empty spools. A spool with a cardboard top made a very nice table. We didn't have many fancy toys back then, but with our active imaginations we didn't really need them.

Here Comes the Mailman

In 1902, when S.J. "Sam" Ellington Sr. started delivering the mail in Summerfield, not a single mile of his mail route was paved.

Maybe it's good that he was driving a buggy at the time. Not only were the roads unpaved, only two of the thirty-one miles he traveled were graded roads. Wonder how many times he got stuck in the mud after he started driving a mail wagon. He also wore out eight Ford cars during his thirty years as a mail carrier.

When he first started, none of his patrons subscribed to a daily paper. Most of the mail consisted of tax notices and occasional letters from family members who were away from home.

Mr. Ellington knew all the people on his route and did many things besides delivering the mail. He could advise them from which mail-order house they could order the various articles they needed and helped fill out order blanks for everything from baby rattles to tractors. Thus he knew what girl had a new dress, and he also knew where she got it and how much she paid for it. Most of the time, he knew why she bought it, whether for a party, a wedding or some other occasion.

The women on his route could tell by his smile if a long-awaited letter had come, and his was usually the first word of sympathy when bad news came with the mailbag.

During World War I, his load was heavier with mail from local boys in foreign countries and with Liberty bonds and savings stamps. But he claimed that his busiest days were before the enactment of the Eighteenth Amendment. Orders poured through the mail for liquor for Saturday night socials and old-time corn shuckings, and perhaps some of it was for medicinal purposes. At one time, liquor orders were so numerous that the postal inspector was sent to Summerfield to investigate the reason for the abnormal number of money orders from such a small post office.

Mr. Ellington's daughter Mae started driving while still in her teens and sometimes carried the mail for him, probably in an unofficial capacity.

With the development of parcel post, his mail car became a veritable department store, delivering everything from queen bees and day-old chicks to engagement rings and automobile tires. Mr. Ellington said that the only thing he ever refused to deliver was a highly overripe crab. Someone on vacation at the beach had thought to surprise the folks back home with something unusual from the coast.

Samuel J. Ellington Sr. was the mail carrier for thirty years. *Courtesy Kay E. Bennett.*

John H. Barker's store, later operated by Samuel J. Ellington Sr. Mr. Barker is standing on the porch. *Courtesy the museum at Summerfield Town Hall.*

When he retired in 1932, D.E. Morgan, Ellington's successor on the mail route, honored him with a Brunswick stew from the patrons of Summerfield R.F.D. No. 2. A.C. Metz gave a speech of appreciation. As a lasting token of his patrons' affection, Ellington was presented with a handsome armchair, footstool and a smoking stand to match.

Mr. Ellington wasn't ready for complete retirement, though. He bought a store that was formerly operated by John Barker near the railroad depot on what is now Summerfield Road. It was called the Poplar Grocery, and the post office was located in a room on the side of the building. Dewey Trogdon remembers that there was a Shell gas pump at the store.

Mr. Ellington carried a few groceries, hoop cheese, a little thread and some cloth. He also had a long glass counter filled with candy, some of it penny candy, and snacks. After school, some of the children would stop by the store to buy candy. Dewey also remembers that for five cents you could get a drink, called a 3-Center, and two Moon Pies. Fertilizer and feed were stored in the back room of the store. Dewey remembers loading sacks of feed for people in the late 1930s. He also remembers that Billie Stafford worked in the store after school.

Some of the people probably gathered in the store to catch up on local and national news, so Mr. Ellington didn't completely lose touch with his former mail patrons.

Miss Kate Was Town's Historian Extraordinaire

Mary Katherine Hoskins, or "Miss Kate," as she was affectionately called, loved history. Born July 25, 1893, she could have gotten her love of history from her father, Joseph A. Hoskins, who was also a history buff. He was a Guilford County sheriff and was said to be the last "hanging sheriff" in the county. One of his granddaughters said that, according to family tradition, Joseph Hoskins was so upset because of the one and only time that he had to pull the rope for a hanging that he never ran for sheriff again.

Kate's sister, "Miss Nelle," kept up with the family history. Kate once said that if she had trouble going to sleep, she'd ask Nelle to recite the family lineage. That would put her to sleep every time!

Kate probably attended the old Brick School in Summerfield; her brothers and a sister also went to school there. She later attended the State Normal and Industrial College, now University of North Carolina–Greensboro. She taught for a short time at a one-room school in Thomasville. I'll bet she made history come alive for her students.

Katherine "Miss Kate" Hoskins was for many years the town historian. *Courtesy Frances S. Welborn.*

In 1933, Kate and Nelle narrowly escaped death when their house burned down. When the fire was discovered in a downstairs room, they ran upstairs to try to save some of their personal belongings. The sisters became trapped by the flames and smoke and might have perished if not for the quick thinking and action of A.C. Metz, the principal of Summerfield High School, and other neighbors. They put a ladder up to one of the windows and brought down Kate and the unconscious Nelle.

Miss Kate loved telling schoolchildren about Summerfield history. She told them about Charles Bruce, supposedly the first white man in what is now Summerfield, and about the American Indians who were here before him. She told them that the muster ground was on the site of the school, now Summerfield Elementary School.

She also enjoyed sharing stories about James Gillies, "Lighthorse Harry" Lee's unarmed bugle boy who was killed by the British. At one of her storytelling sessions, she joined a first-grade class for a lunch of stone soup. Joanne Caldwell was the teacher at the time; she washed a stone and put it in the pot and then added carrots, potatoes, barley and possibly beef that the children had brought. The children were dressed as Indians and early settlers.

Evidently, Miss Kate's stories made quite an impression on the students. One of the school newspapers, appropriately named the *Bugler*, was started in 1938. And when the first school yearbook was published in 1948, it was called *Bugle Notes*—the newspaper and yearbook probably got their names because of Miss Kate's stories.

She helped get a marker for the Bruce family cemetery and wrote many history articles for the *Greensboro Daily News* and *Our State* magazine. What a shame that she never wrote a book about Summerfield.

Known for her wonderful sense of humor, in her later years Miss Kate and some friends traveled to England and other countries. While in London, she went out alone one day to buy something. She and a Londoner struck up a conversation, and she told him that she wished she could attend a session of Parliament. He offered to take her, but her group wasn't going to remain in London that long. She went back to the hotel room and told the other ladies, "Well, I might be old, but I'm not too old to get propositioned!" Though she never married, she once told a friend, "People say poor Miss Kate never married, but poor Miss Kate never found a man she wanted to marry."

She teased the Welborn children, Rusty, Randy, Mike and Annette, by telling them that she was a witch. One day, after having an automatic door opener installed in her garage, she visited the Jack and Frances Welborn family across the street. "I told you I was a witch," she said to the children, "and I'll prove it. Watch the garage door. It's going to open." And to their amazement, it did—with the help of the remote control in Miss Kate's pocket.

Kate had many other interests in addition to her love of history. She took over much of the family farming operation and was a land and forestry conservationist. She also developed Elmhurst Estates, probably the first housing development in Summerfield. Elmhurst had been the name of the family farm. She incorporated some family names into the street names: Joseph Hoskins Road, Dickinben Drive, Sarelma Drive, Pauline Court and possibly others.

Miss Kate died February 22, 1986, at Friends Homes in Greensboro. We owe her a tremendous debt of gratitude for preserving so much of our Summerfield history.

Local Boy Becomes Surgeon, Inventor

His first job paid ten cents per week. But that was more than one hundred years ago, when Herbert H. Ogburn was just a young boy. He grew up on a farm, and his job was milking the cow morning and night, seven days a week. Maybe milking the cow strengthened his fingers for his surgical work later in life.

Dr. Herbert H. Ogburn. *Courtesy Jean Ogburn Hattle and Sallie Ogburn Houck.*

Herbert Ogburn was born in 1886, the son of the Reverend Thomas J. and Nannie Davidson Ogburn. With his family, he attended Flat Rock Methodist Church. The trip to church was quite an adventure. His uncle, Lee Ogburn, would send his two-horse covered wagon for their ride to church. The road was rough, with many large rocks and deep mudholes. Chairs were placed on the wagon for the women and older people, but the children

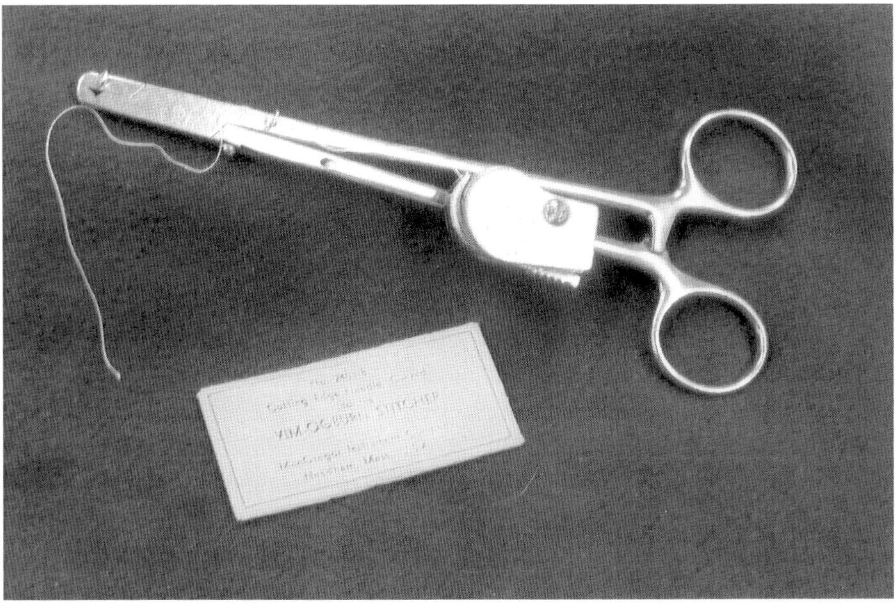

Surgical stitcher invented by Dr. Herbert H. Ogburn. *Courtesy Greensboro Medical Historical Library, Moses Cone Health System.*

rode on the brake or in the feed box on the rear of the wagon—that way they could hop on and off the wagon when they got tired of riding. At church, the horses and mules were tied to tree limbs, and everybody greeted friends and neighbors before entering the church.

Herbert Ogburn was a student at the old Brick School at Summerfield and the Summerfield Academy and Business Institute before attending Oak Ridge Institute. He also attended Lafayette College and the University of North Carolina and graduated in surgery from Johns Hopkins Medical School. In 1962, he was awarded a medal for being a fifty-year practicing alumnus of that school.

During World War I, he served with a medical unit in France near the battlefield of Verdun. He was discharged as a lieutenant colonel. Later he became superintendent at Wesley Long Community Hospital, and it was said that the records he kept were among the best in the United States. When the hospital went bankrupt, he and eleven others bought it and kept it going.

His brother, Roger Ogburn, also became a doctor. His career was cut short when he went on an ambulance call one night in 1927 in New York City. He was killed when the ambulance was hit by a car driven by a drunk driver.

Pauline Robinson remembers being told about Dr. Herbert Ogburn performing surgery on her grandfather Burgess "Byrd" Johnson about 1924. Mr. Johnson was about eighty-four or eighty-five years old and had a strangulated hernia. The surgery was performed on the kitchen table at Johnson's house, and whiskey was used as an anesthetic. The surgery was a success, and Johnson lived until he was eighty-seven.

In addition to being a well-known surgeon, Dr. Ogburn also became an inventor. While observing operations at Charity Hospital in New Orleans in 1943, he was struck by the thought that there was much lost motion in the continual threading and rethreading of surgical needles. He decided that much time would be saved if a device were available so that the needle would remain threaded. He returned to his hotel and by morning had drawn plans for his idea.

In less than a year after returning to Greensboro, and with the help of Sam H. Patton, the first model was in working order. A bobbin was added to a regular needle holder. Dr. Ogburn applied for patent rights in December 1943 and later applied for a patent in England. He demonstrated the surgical stitcher for a group of medical officials in Chicago. The stitcher was used in the United States, as well as in England, Canada and South America. In recognition of his invention, he was given a plaque by the Guilford County Medical Society.

Some of Dr. Ogburn's other inventions included a hospital bed on which the head could be cranked up, a coffin, a medicine to stop motion sickness and restraints for combative patients. He made notable contributions to surgical techniques, gaining international recognition.

He married Bobbie Jean Truesdale, and they had two daughters, Jean and Sallie. Dr. Ogburn died on December 21, 1964, at age seventy-eight. Did he ever dream, while he was milking the cow back on the farm, that he would accomplish so much during his lifetime?

Scrap Sketches Were Her Specialty

Hilda Lanier Ogburn (1895–1984) grew up in the Summerfield area. She was a member of a very talented family; two of her brothers, Herbert and Roger, were doctors, and her sister, Bess Whitaker, was a musician who gave piano lessons to many Oak Ridge and Summerfield children.

Hilda L. Ogburn with some of her scrap sketches. *Courtesy Jean Ogburn Hattle and Sallie Ogburn Houck.*

Hilda probably attended the old Brick School in Summerfield; she was in a photograph of the students there even before she was old enough to be in school. She later attended Converse College in

Spartanburg, South Carolina, and studied at the Art Students League in New York City, of which she was a lifetime member. She was also a charter member of the Altrusa Club.

For several years, she worked for the Works Project Administration, better known as the WPA. She illustrated a book published by the WPA, titled *A Bundle of Troubles and Other Tar Heel Tales*. She was supervisor of teaching at the Greensboro Art Center in 1936 and for several years after. Examples of children's art completed under her direction were chosen for exhibitions of children's work throughout the country.

In March 1938, she was appointed assistant director of the center while Frederick Whiteman was the director. As well as teaching art, she gave talks for school groups. A lecture for the seventh grades of Central and Caldwell Schools included 125 boys and girls. Some of the art discussed was from the collection of Mrs. John D. Rockefeller Jr.

When an art center was opened in Greenville, North Carolina, in 1939, Miss Ogburn was employed as the full-time director. Her duties included scheduling art exhibitions, art classes and art appreciation lectures.

Over the years, she worked in oils and watercolors and sold many of her paintings. While she had an upstairs studio at the corner of Elm and Market Streets in Greensboro, she made numerous sketches of pedestrians passing by. Most of her sketches were of black people. She said that the Southern blacks had an emotional appeal for her, and she dared the viewer to see anything critical in any of her pictures.

She had a portfolio full of sketches but couldn't quite decide the best way to use them. She did an oil painting from one sketch, which was bought by the Town of Hickory, North Carolina, for its art gallery's permanent collection, and later did a scrap sketch from the same original. Years went by before she felt that she had discovered the perfect medium for her sketches. While on a trip to Mexico City, she had purchased some plaques. The plaques later inspired her scrap sketches, which became her unique niche in the art world.

She only needed simple supplies for her scrap sketches: black construction paper, India ink, Elmer's glue and cuticle scissors, along with scraps of fabric. But she also needed a lot of artistic ability.

Her first scrap sketch was sold to Mrs. W.Y. Preyer Jr. in 1956 for the Preyers' mountain home at Roaring Gap. Miss Ogburn kept records of those who purchased her scrap sketches. Oscar Mayer, the meatpacker, bought five of them. A man from Tennessee bought eighteen because he thought they would become collectors' items. The McNeill Smiths bought one for a French boy who had lived with them as an exchange student. Several people in Summerfield are lucky enough to own one of her scrap sketches.

Her scrap sketches can be found in nineteen states and in the Smithsonian Institution, as well as in places as far away as Paris and London. Appropriately enough, four of them are in the Greensboro Historical Museum collection but are not currently on display. The museum is located not far from where many of her sketches were drawn so many years ago.

CADET NURSES SHARE FOND MEMORIES

During World War II, the nation was facing a nursing shortage. So many nurses were in the military that there were not enough left for civilian needs. So in July 1943, the Cadet Nurse Corps was established under the administration of the United States Public Health Service. Hospitals with schools of nursing that met the standards of the Health Service were allowed to train nurses as part of the corps. St. Leo's Hospital in Greensboro was one of those.

Ruby Lee Jessup in Cadet Nurse Corps uniform, including overcoat. *Courtesy Ruby Jessup Groce.*

The Cadet Corps had gray and white seersucker uniforms for summer and gray wool suits with long overcoats for winter. Those uniforms were only worn for special occasions. The working uniform was white, and after six months'

Ila Scarlette in Cadet Nurse Corps uniform. *Courtesy Ila Scarlette Ingold.*

training, they received a white cap. At graduation, they received black bands on the caps.

The rules at St. Leo's were strict. Rings, nail polish and excessive cosmetics could not be worn while in uniform. Students had to clean their own rooms and were required to report for classes and lectures in complete uniform, even if they were off duty. Curfew was 10:00 p.m. The housemother, Mrs. Morgan, did a bed check every night to be sure that all students were in their beds.

The training lasted three years with a week's vacation the first year, two weeks the second year and three weeks the third year. The amount of pay the students received is uncertain; it could have been ten dollars per month the first year, fifteen dollars the second year and twenty dollars the third year.

St. Leo's normally didn't have children as patients; they were usually taken to Sternberger Hospital. Although some of the students did some training at Sternberger, most went to Children's Hospital in Washington, D.C., for three months of pediatric training. Three months of psychiatric training took place at Dix Hill Hospital in Raleigh, North Carolina, or at a hospital in Baltimore, Maryland.

Helen Jones Angel remembers that on her third day of training, she went on duty in the hospital; she only did things like getting water or bedpans for the patients. The nurses had to attend classes and work on the floor also. Before going on duty, all the students were required to attend chapel. St. Leo's was operated by the Sisters of Charity, but all the nurses said that they were never pressured to convert to Catholicism.

Kate Lee Robinson was the cadet nurse who liked to skate in the halls of the nurses' home while in training. *Courtesy Ruby Jessup Groce.*

The students worked hard and studied harder, but they still had enough energy left to have fun. Sometimes Sister Vincent, the superintendent of nursing, would dance with the students; they had a jukebox in the living room of the nurses' home. At times, she would call the priest at ORD (the army's Overseas Replacement Depot), and he would send over GIs for dances. Sister Vincent, along with the housemother, chaperoned the dances.

Since ORD was close by, the students got to know some of the GIs. Occasionally, a few of them would drop by the nurses' home, and at times some of the girls upstairs would pass notes, tied to a string, down to the soldiers and they'd pass notes back!

Poor Mrs. Morgan, who was called "Gram" by the students, really earned her salary as housemother! Keeping check on all those girls was quite a chore. When there was a blackout, the girls would put on high-heeled shoes and run up and down the halls. They were upstairs and "Gram" was downstairs; she probably dreaded blackouts!

Cadet nurses with black bands on their caps. *Left to right:* Ruby Pegram, Helen Jones, Nita Bull and Annie Mae Brendle. Is that a diploma in Ruby's hand? *Courtesy Helen Jones Angel.*

Kate Lee Robinson used to roller-skate in the halls, and when somebody warned her that one of the Sisters was coming, she'd skate into the nearest room and hide in the closet. Some of the nurses said later that they thought the Sister would jingle her keys so they'd know she was coming.

I wonder how many of the students got in the clothes hamper to hide from the Sisters until they could get upstairs to their rooms. And how many sneaked out after curfew to go uptown to a diner near the intersection of Summit Avenue and Church Street. They'd walk to the diner and get something to eat, and then some of the soldiers would walk back with them. Lamb stew was served to the students very often and was not a favorite dish. Maybe that's why they sneaked out to go to the diner, or maybe it was because they knew there would be GIs there.

Between 1943 and 1948, over 124,000 nurses graduated from the Cadet Nurse Corps. We can be proud that some of our own girls were among that number. Helen Jones, Ruby Pegram, Kate Lee Robinson, Ruby Lee Jessup and Ila Scarlette, all from Summerfield, were in the Cadet Nurse Corps, along with Annie Mae Brendle from Oak Ridge and Margaret Flynt and Frances and Burneda Simpson from Stokesdale.

Thanks to all the cadet nurses who shared their memories.

HE WAS A FRIEND TO ALL

His name was Jarvis Mitchell, but to most people in Summerfield he was known simply as Gufas (rhymes with "cuff-us"). Gufas (1890–1987) was the son of Thomas and Isabell Mitchell. He was well known and well liked by everybody, especially children.

Sammy Angel remembers walking over to the Mitchell House when he was about five years old. Gufas's wife, Gertrude, would always give him something to eat, even if it was just a jelly biscuit. Barbara Angel Cockman remembers him telling stories to the children.

Mildred Pope, along with Barbara, Betty and Sarah Lee Perdue, were out playing in the yard one day. Gufas came by, driving his wagon, and asked them if they wanted to ride. Of course they said yes and hopped up on the wagon. When they got back home, Mildred got a good spanking and the Perdue girls got a good scolding—they hadn't bothered to ask

Jarvis "Gufas" Mitchell was truly a friend to all. *Courtesy David H. Angel.*

their mamas if they could go! Donnie Perdue once remarked that when Gufas hauled hay, he had more children on the wagon than he did hay.

When David Angel was small, his grandmother was sick and needed a lot of care. Gufas would come by and tell Clara, David's mother, that he'd take David and look after him for a while so she could get some rest. He took David to ride on the wagon, and it was a real treat if Gufas took him to the drugstore and bought him a cherry smash.

David remembers going to the Mitchell House. As well as the usual chickens and turkeys, they had a peacock. They also had at least two big boxwoods in the yard, and one was always trimmed into the shape of a chair.

Clyde Robinson Jr. sometimes helped Gufas with tobacco. They ate lunch outside, and Gertrude kept the flies away from the food with a small branch from a tree.

Bill Gordon remembers that he and Gufas used to pitch horseshoes between Gordon's store and Jesse Winfree's store. When Gufas won, he enjoyed yelling to Bill, "Pitch, loser!" Bill enjoyed squirrel hunting but always gave the squirrels to Gufas. Fried squirrel and gravy was a tasty dish.

Gufas was a farmer and plowed many gardens for neighbors. He was a chauffer for the Caesar Cone family for several years; he might have started when they still traveled by buggy. One year at Christmas, R.C. Gordon hired Gufas to chauffer the Gordon family to Greensboro to see the Christmas lights.

Gufas had a trash-hauling business, using his pickup truck. Perry Pass and his father helped him, and later Perry's father took over the business. Babe Martin and Gufas raised turkeys and had turkey shoots in the fall at Gufas's farm.

On Saturday nights, Gufas, along with other people, would gather at Gordon's store and talk and eat sardines or Vienna sausages. Mr. Gordon kept salt and pepper under the counter to go with them. Once in a while, Mr. Gordon would have a drawing for a prize. Peggy Simpson Doss remembers drawing the names, or numbers, from a hat for the winner, and Mr. Gordon always gave her a candy bar. Sometimes, he'd sprinkle some salt on the floor and get Bob Parrish to dance it into the oiled wood. He'd give Bob a can or two of sardines and some crackers, and Bob would dance up a storm.

All of the Brittain boys had fond memories of Gufas. Bill Brittain said that after his father died, Gufas tried to keep an eye on the boys. Bill said that one day when he did something Gufas didn't approve of, he told Bill, "You know your daddy wouldn't want you to do that." Bob Brittain remembers that he and Gufas went by Guy Ayers's watermelon patch and decided to sample the melons. Just after they left the watermelon patch, they got too close to a yellow jacket nest. Gufas got stung and Bob got covered with stings. Was that their payback for getting into the watermelons? They had probably already gotten Guy's OK before they got any of the melons.

Herbert Scarlette said that Gufas went to Lynch's Lodge one night. While he was inside, some of the boys lifted the back of his Model A Ford and put watermelon rinds under the tires. When Gufas started to leave, the car wouldn't move! He walked on home, which was nearby, and went back the next day and saw what they had done. Wonder how long it took for him to get the joke back on them.

Herbert also remembered that one day Gufas's mules ran away; they went down Oak Ridge Road and ran up on the porch of Gordon's store. The posts of the porch stopped the wagon. When Gufas came walking down the road to get them, he said he knew they'd stop somewhere. It's a good thing there was a lot less traffic then.

Our family used to gather around the piano and sing on Sunday night after church. Sometimes Gufas would come and sing with us. He had a beautiful baritone voice and sang in the choir at Peace Church. He also sang many solos at church and for funerals. What a legacy…to be remembered as everybody's friend.

Summerfield Junior Order and Daughters of America

The Summerfield Council of the Junior Order of United American Mechanics was organized in Summerfield on May 25, 1905, when twenty-six members were initiated by the Oak Ridge Junior Order Council, according to the *Greensboro Patriot.* The charter members were shown on the Junior Order Charter: S.W. Allred, R.W. Burton, B.Z. Byrd, J.P. Calhoun, J.W. Case, G.H. Deboe, F.W. Doggett, J.C. Doggett, T.B. Doggett, S.J. Ellington, J.R. Hoskins, W.D. Lane, J.F. Medearis, N.W. Ogburn, J.B. Smith, T.J. Smith, H.J. Wilson, J.A. Wilson, J.W. Winchester, G.F. Winfree, D.C. Wright and Robert Wright. Only twenty-two members were listed on the charter.

The Junior Order members presented a flag and Bible to the school in November 1905. This must have been the old Brick School or the Summerfield Academy and Business Institute since the two-story high school wasn't built until several years later.

In August 1906, the *Greensboro Patriot* reported that "the Junior Order is fitting up a hall over Mr. N.W. Ogburn's store." Mr. Ogburn owned and operated the G.J. Smith store, which is now known as Gordon's Hardware Store.

It's not known when the Junior Hall was moved to the Brittain Store building. Evidently, they rented the space from the person who was running the store for many years. Lionel Alley said that the Juniors had the steps built on the side of the store building about 1937. Before that they had to go through the store to get to the Junior Hall upstairs.

Junior Order members sometime before September 21, 1931. *Seated, left to right*: Percy Highfill, John Tilley, Samuel J. Ellington Sr., Henry Thorpe and T.D. Alley. *Standing, left to right*: James Proctor, Clark Doggett, O.C. Brown, Ed Boswell, Charlie Dye, Garrett Parrish and Lee Tilley. *Courtesy Edna Tilley.*

Summerfield residents enjoyed a free ice cream supper given by the Junior Order in August 1913. The organization served cake and ice cream to a large crowd in the grove near Wilson's store. That would have been between the town hall parking lot and Highway 220.

A Bible and flag were presented to the new brick school in May 1925. J.D. Preston of Stokesdale, Reverend Mr. Dawson, Professor T.R. Foust and L.B. Mendenhall, of Greensboro, all had a part in the program.

The Junior Order had lots of oyster stews. Lucian Parrish and T.D. Alley were the chief cooks. The Juniors bought five gallons of oysters and two pounds of butter; the members who owned cows furnished the milk. The stews were cooked on a kerosene stove, and the members kept dishes at the Junior Hall so they didn't have to carry dishes back and forth. An oil lamp used by the Junior Order is now in the small museum located in the town hall.

Juniors everywhere must have liked oyster stew; in 1935, the Junior Council of Revolution invited the Summerfield Council to an oyster stew—"Revolution" likely referring to the Revolution Mill area of Greensboro.

A program honoring the eleven districts was held at Summerfield in May 1935. The program included talks by Juniors from Lexington, a play by girls and boys from the Lexington Orphanage, songs by the Summerfield High School choir, a moving picture show and string music by four boys and a girl from near Hillsdale. About four hundred people were present.

When the tornado struck Greensboro in 1936, the Summerfield Junior Order contributed seventeen dollars to aid those who had been left homeless by the tornado.

Officers elected in 1943 were W.W. Doggett, H.L. Johnson, W.T. Davenport, T.D. Alley, R.L. Tilley, C.C. Pearman, W.D. Davis, C.L. Dye, L.M. Parrish, H.W. Strader and J.C. Moore. The date the Summerfield Council was disbanded is unknown, but it was still active in 1946.

The Daughters of America was the ladies' order of the Junior Order. The Summerfield Council, Bruce Council No. 14, was organized on Saturday May 26, 1928. The council decided to meet each Thursday evening at eight o'clock.

At a meeting in March 1935, those in attendance were Mr. and Mrs. T.D. Alley, Miss Beatrice Alley, Mr. and Mrs. Frank Iddings, Miss Beulah Iddings, Mr. and Mrs. Charlie Dye, Mrs. Stella Proctor, Mrs. Beulah Pegram, Mrs. Francis Friddle, Mrs. Mabel Durham, Mrs. Mary Thorpe, Mrs. Mary Kiger, Miss Mary Winfree, R.O. Gamble, Mrs. Nellie Sherrill and Mrs. Eunice Royster.

Meetings were usually held at the Junior Hall, upstairs in the Brittain Store building, now the Summerfield Town Hall.

The group had monthly birthday suppers for the members and sometimes had oyster suppers. In 1942, the members made a quilt, which they donated to the Junior Order Children's Home in Lexington. All of the members were urged to buy bonds and stamps during World War II. The council was disbanded in June 1971.

"Use It Up, Wear It Out…"

"Use it up, wear it out, make it do, or do without." We didn't hear those words quoted when we were growing up, but our parents, and most everybody in Summerfield, lived by that philosophy.

We'd never heard of recycling, but we did plenty of it. On washday, the water from the wringer washing machine, as well as the water in the rinsing tubs, was carried in buckets to water the flowers or any new shrubbery or trees that needed to be watered.

All food scraps as well as fruit and vegetable peelings were used to feed the dogs, cats, pigs and chickens. We never bought cat food or dog food. Daddy took corn to the mill to be ground into flour, cornmeal or feed for the horses, cows and chickens.

When a chicken was killed for Sunday dinner, the small feathers were saved, washed and dried. These were used to make pillows or, many years ago, feather ticks for the beds. These went on top of straw ticks and really kept people warm in cold weather. It took a long time to save enough feathers to make a feather tick; I guess that's why lots of people left "feather beds" to relatives in their wills many years ago. Mama always saved a few of the larger feathers to oil the sewing machine with.

All the food scraps that weren't given to the dogs, cats and chickens went into the "slop bucket" for the pigs. I think we gave the pigs corncobs left from cutting off corn or from corn on the cob. The pigs gobbled it up like it was good. We even recycled leaves in the fall. We bagged them up in guano sacks and put them in a dry place to be used later in the little shed inside the pigpen for the pigs. The leaves kept them warm during the winter.

Even the manure from the horses, mules and chickens was recycled. Before fertilizer was used widely, the manure from the stables went onto some of the big fields. Nobody had to tell you that the men had been spreading manure that day—your nose told you. The chicken manure was used in the garden and around the flowers.

People saved seeds from vegetables, watermelons and more. Mama had a green thumb and loved to grow flowers. A long time ago, nobody bought flower seeds or plants. Neighbors shared seeds or plants with one another; I've heard them say that if you said "thank you" for the plants, they wouldn't grow.

At church, the flowers were almost always homegrown. At the Baptist church, Mrs. Lela Carter usually arranged her own flowers or occasionally flowers from the garden of someone else. She always did such a good job. I remember one Thanksgiving when she used a hollowed-out pumpkin and filled it with flowers and leaves. It must have been unusually pretty; it stood out in my memory.

Even the Sears catalogue was recycled. After you got a new catalogue, the old one went to the outhouse to be used as toilet paper. If you had newspapers, they were used the same way.

The newspapers and Sears catalogues were recycled in outhouses like this one. *Courtesy Frances Angel.*

Clothes were passed down to the next younger child until they were too ragged to patch or wear. Then the buttons were cut off, and the scraps of material were used for patches or rags. The best scraps went into quilts, which kept us warm during the winter. You could look at the quilts and remember which scraps came from a dress you had worn.

The buttons that were cut off garments were saved in Mama's button can. Different people used different things to keep buttons in. I think Mama's was a gallon-sized lard can. Sometimes the buttons were used over and over for new dresses or shirts. If a button was missing from a shirt or dress, you went to the button can to find a matching one. Sometimes it had to be a near match!

A few years ago, I made Christmas gifts for my family from buttons that came from Mama's button can. I glued buttons onto calico material in the shape of the first initial of the last name of all my brothers and sisters and married nieces and nephews. They were framed in shadow box frames so they all had some of Mama's buttons to keep—and the buttons were recycled once more.

SUMMERFIELD AREA FURNISHES SHERIFFS FOR OVER SEVENTY-FIVE YEARS

Was Joseph Hoskins the first Guilford County sheriff from the Summerfield area? It's possible that some of the earlier sheriffs were also from this area. One possibility is William Moore, who was sheriff in 1771. Was he the Colonel William Moore who was fined fifty pounds for contempt of court in Randolph County for riding his horse into the courthouse while court was in session?

In Guilford County deed records, Joseph Hoskins is shown as constable in 1787, and in 1788 he is shown as deputy sheriff. In 1790, 1794 and 1796, he's shown as sheriff and in 1797 as deputy sheriff again.

James Doak served as sheriff from 1825 through 1846. His grave site has been preserved in the current Ridgewood Subdivision, which is located off Highway 150 West. Our current mayor, Mark Brown, was instrumental in getting the site preserved.

Joseph A. Hoskins served for six years as sheriff according to his obituary. The records indicate that he was sheriff in 1888, 1894 and 1896 and

Sheriff Joseph A. Hoskins. He was the second Sheriff Joseph Hoskins. *Courtesy the Hoskins family.*

deputy sheriff for three years. Was he the grandson of the first sheriff Joseph Hoskins? He was the father of Katherine, Nelle, Richard and Ben Hoskins. In January 1896, the *Greensboro Patriot* reported: "Sheriff Hoskins is looking after the spiritual as well as the temporal welfare of the prisoners in the county jail. Yesterday he distributed among the county's charges a number of religious books and tracts."

The second Joseph Hoskins was said to have taken part in a double hanging that took place at what is now (or was in 1985) the North Carolina A&T University Athletic Field. According to family tradition, he became so upset over the hanging that he wouldn't run for the office again.

Robert M. Stafford served as sheriff from 1865 through 1880. During his tenure, both the jail and the courthouse burned down. When the courthouse burned, most of the books, papers and more were saved.

Thirty-two years later, his son, David B. Stafford, was elected sheriff. "Dave" Stafford was born near Summerfield and attended a one-room log school at Ridgefield and later Oak Ridge Military Academy. He was a farmer and country store owner in Oak Ridge in 1910 when he decided that he wanted to become sheriff. He traveled in his buggy to many, if not all, of the townships, asking people to vote for him. He wasn't elected that year, but two years later he won the election and remained as sheriff for twenty years.

Sheriff Dave waged a war on bootleggers and even arrested people he'd known from boyhood. He remarked that his one rule was "to follow one's duty, regardless of friends, foes or politics." After thirteen years in office, he said he'd never been fired upon, and his obituary stated that he didn't once fire upon another human being.

One night, when he had a Negro man as a prisoner, he heard that a mob might come to the jail. He took the prisoner to another part of the courthouse and sat down to watch, wait and guard. He said later that he was bound to protect the prisoner to the same extent as any other man, and he was going to do it or find himself trying. Thankfully, the mob never arrived. Someone asked him later where he hid the prisoner. He wouldn't tell the location; he said he might need to use it again.

In earlier years, one of the duties of the sheriff was to collect taxes. During Sheriff Dave's first year in office, he collected about $275,000, but in his last year in office about $2 million dollars was collected. His hardest duty was to eject a family, but he said that if no one was ill, he had no choice but to put them out.

Many of the sheriff's deputies have also come from the Summerfield area. Among them are Robert Alsup Stafford, Lee Stafford, John H. Barker, Gurney Long, Austin Tuttle, John Wray, Mark Brown, David Thacker, Mike Bennett, Billy Case and John Daniel. There were possibly others.

Our present sheriff, B.J. Barnes, wasn't born in Summerfield but was living here when he became sheriff in 1994. During his tenure, he was nominated for National Sheriff of the Year, and the Guilford County Sheriff's Department was named the best large department in North Carolina by the Governor's Crime Commission.

For over seventy-five years, the Summerfield area has furnished Guilford County sheriffs. Could there be another sheriff from Summerfield sometime in the future?

THANKSGIVING MEMORIES: FOR THOSE, WE GIVE THANKS

I don't remember going to Grandma's house for Thanksgiving dinner—but I do remember going to birthday dinners for my Grandma Parrish. They were held outside under the trees, and sometimes somebody would shoo away the flies with a small tree limb. All her children, grandchildren, great-grandchildren and other family members attended.

Lydia Parrish, wearing a bonnet, at her birthday dinner about 1939. *Courtesy Mildred Pope Jessup.*

My nieces and nephews have fond memories of going to Grandma's or Granny's for Thanksgiving. Everybody would gather at our house, and we always had lots of good food. Mama would cook a huge turkey and make several pans of dressing. She didn't stuff the turkey; we all liked the dressing spread thinly in big pans and cooked very brown in the oven. At one time, Mama and Marvin, one of my brothers, raised turkeys, but later the turkeys came from the grocery store.

Mama always made a huge bowl of mashed potatoes and cooked several big pans of homemade biscuits. With eight children, she'd had lots of practice making biscuits over the years. They were so good, especially when they were cooked in the old wood-burning stove; later she used an electric stove. We had all kinds of vegetables, most of them homegrown and either canned or frozen by the time Thanksgiving came around.

All my sisters and sisters-in-law were good cooks. Instead of each one cooking just one dish, they fixed a complete meal so they'd have leftovers for supper. And even with our big family, there were always some leftovers!

Over the years, each cook was expected to bring one or two of the family's favorites. All my sisters-in-law were Angels and cooked heavenly food! Frances Angel cooked the best corn, and we all looked forward to her brown sugar pies, pound cakes and pickles. Lib Angel made delicious potato salad, cranberry salad and German chocolate cake. Rachel Angel didn't dare show up without her fresh coconut cake, candied yams and turnips.

Lucille Pope, my oldest sister, cooked squash casserole, hypocrite pies and fried apple pies. Lib Nelson, another sister, was noted for her chocolate pies and had to bring four or five of them to keep people from fighting over the last piece. One year, somebody hid a whole pie, but they didn't get away with it for long. My sister, Ila Ingold, makes the best-ever banana cake and still brings it to our family Christmas dinners. My younger sister, Hilda Pegram, makes sweet potato casserole that's as good as any dessert.

Sometimes the men would saw wood, go hunting or play horseshoes while the women were putting the finishing touches to the meal and the children played outside. When everything was done, all the family was rounded up and the blessing was asked. We didn't go around the table to tell what we were thankful for, but we were thankful for so many things, especially family. We didn't have paper plates for many years, and the men would all sit down and eat first. Then the children ate, and—at last!—the women sat down to eat. That way, the women could sit and relax, eat, talk and enjoy their meal. Sometimes my brother "Jap" would stay in the kitchen to refill tea and coffee for the women. Of course, there were a lot of dishes to wash, but with so many to help, it wasn't such a big chore. Usually, while the men and children were eating, most of the pots and pans were washed and sorted out.

In later years, we used paper plates, cups and plastic forks; we all stood up if we couldn't find a place to sit, and the children would sometimes sit on the stair steps to eat. If the weather wasn't too cold, some of the men would eat outside at the picnic table.

After the meal, the children would play in the barn, or sometimes some of the adults and children would play ball in the cow pasture—but you had to watch where you put your feet. We no longer get together for Thanksgiving, but most of our family still enjoy getting together at Christmas, and we still have lots to be thankful for.

She Was One Busy Lady

Florence Shelton was born in Patrick County, Virginia, in 1875. She married Andrew Jackson Ayers, and they moved to Summerfield about 1916. Their family grew to include ten children (six boys and four girls). Some of the children had some unusual nicknames: "Goat," "Green" and "Blue."

You'd think that cooking, canning, cleaning, doing laundry and looking after ten children would keep a mother too busy to even think about any community activities. But that wasn't true for Mrs. Ayers.

Florence Ayers was a very busy lady. *Courtesy Linda Ayers Southard.*

Mr. and Mrs. Ayers were charter members of the Summerfield Grange when it was organized in 1930. Mrs. Ayers was also active in and a frequent hostess for the Tongue and Needle Club and the Home Demonstration Club. She was also a member of the Woman's Missionary Union at Summerfield Baptist Church.

She must have loved entertaining people in her home. For many years, she prepared an annual dinner for the entire school faculty. This was probably a highlight of the year for the teachers and was thoroughly enjoyed. She was a member of the school committee during the 1923–24 school year and possibly for other years.

She knew most of the teachers well since many of them boarded at the Ayers home over the years. In 1927, A.C. Metz, Misses Morgan, Green, Linker and Sandlin and Mrs. Martin were all boarders there. That meant a lot of extra cooking and cleaning. One of the last boarders in the Ayers home was Harold Cook, a highway patrolman.

At one time, the telephone central office was located at the Ayers home. All the members of the family must have been expected to help with the operation. Dura Mae Ayers remembered that her husband, Guy, told her that he hated answering the switchboard and would ring with his toes!

When Mrs. Ayers operated a cloth store in the Brittain Store building, she didn't stay in the store all day. Herbert Scarlette remembered that she had a sign on the door telling people to come to the brick house across the road to get her if they wanted to purchase cloth. Vivian Robinson Morris remembered the cloth store being in the Brittain Building when she worked at the telephone central office at Mrs. Taylor's house from 1940 to 1944.

The cloth store was located in the Ayers home for many years. It occupied the room next to the back porch and had lots of tables with bolts of cloth stacked on them. When the ladies of Summerfield wanted cloth for a new dress for themselves or their children, they didn't have to make a trip to Greensboro. Many of them could just walk to Mrs. Ayers's cloth store and enjoy a visit while they shopped.

I think I remember someone telling me that Mrs. Ayers kept her scissors tied with elastic to one of the tables in the cloth room. If she carried the scissors over to another table to cut cloth and forgot and turned them loose, they'd go flying back!

Barbara Ayers Trogdon remembers some of the local ladies going to the cloth store to do their quilting. If they didn't have enough scraps for their quilting, they probably bought the cloth from Mrs. Ayers. In 1940, the *Greensboro Patriot* reported, "Mrs. A.J. Ayers entertained a few of her friends recently with an old-fashioned quilting party. A bountiful dinner was served at noon."

In later years, she enjoyed an occasional outing to Greensboro. She and Mrs. Annie Parrish, along with Mrs. Lee Taylor, rode the "Blue Goose" bus to Greensboro for a day of shopping and lunch at the S&W Cafeteria. Linda Southard remembers her grandmother, Mrs. Ayers, telling that Mrs. Taylor ordered three kinds of potatoes one day!

I wish I could ask her at least one question: where did she find the time, and the energy, for all her various activities at home and in the community?

Summerfield Grange Keeps On Going After Seventy-eight Years

It wasn't the first club or civic organization in Summerfield, but it has survived longer than any of the others. It was organized on February 19, 1930.

The National Grange was first started in 1867 as a nationwide organization to improve the lives of farmers and their families, but the Grange in North Carolina didn't last long. When Harry B. Caldwell led the effort to reorganize the Grange in North Carolina, Summerfield Grange was the first to be organized in Guilford County in 1930. Beginning with 40 charter members in February, the Grange membership had grown to 104 in just one month. R. Flake Shaw was elected as the first Summerfield Grange master, but he resigned shortly after to run for county commissioner, and Richard Ogburn was elected to replace him.

In July 1930, a Grange picnic was held at Guilford Battleground with several hundred people in attendance. Other Grange units from Guilford County included Alamance, Pleasant Garden, Sumner, Nathaniel Greene and Gibsonville. Members from Forsyth and Alamance Counties were also present. C.G. Hunter of Tobaccoville won the horseshoeing contest, and Mrs. J.W. McCorkle of Kernersville won the husband-calling contest. Members of Summerfield Grange won their share of prizes. The T.D. Alley and Doak Winfree families, with nine members each, won prizes for the largest family at the picnic. Mary Lou Robinson won the girls' ball-throwing contest, Marion Ayers won the cake-eating contest and John D. Winfrey came in second in the boys' sack race.

The 1938 annual Grange and Farmers Picnic took place at Summerfield High School. The recreation program began at 5:30 p.m. and the picnic supper at 6:30 p.m. The main program started at 7:30 p.m. in the auditorium with several speakers, a number of vocal selections by the Mothersingers of the Summerfield PTA and solos by Billy Shields, also from Summerfield.

Contest winners at the 1939 picnic received some rather unusual prizes: J.C. Causey, a large milk pail for having the largest family present; Joe Long, of Summerfield, five quarts of motor oil for traveling the greatest distance; Mr. and Mrs. Agans, a gallon of ice cream for being married the longest (fifty years); Mr. and Mrs. Moir Ayers, an alarm clock for being the newest married couple; A.B. Phillippie, a gallon of livestock spray for having operated a farm the longest (forty years); and A.C. Metz and J.C. Causey, toothpaste for bringing the largest number of people.

Summerfield Grange members with Christmas bags prepared for shut-ins in the community. *Left to right*: Linda Hutson, Dorothy Knight, Earline Huffman, Joanne Caldwell, Frances Angel, Anna Lou Preston, Hilda Pegram, Fred Hutson, Lucille Rice, Rebecca Gatewood and Dwight Angel. *Courtesy the author.*

Over the years, the Summerfield Grange has been involved in many efforts to improve the community in a variety of ways. The local, state and national Grange has worked with legislators on the state and national level. The Summerfield Grange has sponsored the Boy Scouts, helped to get a dial telephone system, improved roads, a new post office and the present community center. A few years ago, the Grange took part in the Adopt-a-Highway program, but that project had to be given up.

The Grange, the Civitan Club and the Garden Club cooked country ham suppers, pinto bean suppers and Brunswick stews and held yard sales, quilt raffles and house tours to make money to build the community center.

In recent years, many farms have disappeared, in the Piedmont area especially, so the focus of the Grange has undergone some changes. A statement from a recent issue of *The North Carolina Grange News* sums up the purpose of the Grange: "The Grange is a family-oriented, community service organization, with a special interest in rural and agricultural issues, designed to help meet the needs of people, young and old, through grassroots efforts with our government and other organizations who also seek the greatest good for the greatest number." The Grange motto is "In essentials, unity; in non-essentials, liberty; and in all things charity."

The Summerfield Grange reaches out to the community in various ways. Through a Birthday Club for foster teens, birthday cards and gift cards are sent to the teens on their birthdays. Small luggage is provided to the foster teens each year. All of the Grange units in the state, including Summerfield, collect labels and box tops for education for Gateway Education Center, a school for severely handicapped children in Greensboro. At Easter, bags of Easter eggs, candy, pencils and more are prepared for homeless children. The members enjoy preparing and delivering bags of "goodies" for local shut-ins and elderly people at Christmas. A more recent project involves taking a basket of crackers and other snacks for patients and family members to the Cancer Center in Greensboro. Members are always ready to help when special needs arise.

After seventy-eight years of continuous service, the local Grange is fortunate to have one surviving charter member, O'Dell Highfill. Linda Hutson is the current Grange president. Grange meetings are held on the third Monday night of each month at 7:00 p.m. at the Summerfield Community Center. Visitors and new members are welcome.

Visiting Brings Back Memories for Texas Doctor

William E. Shields, better known locally as Bill or Billy, was born in Summerfield in 1919. His father died when he was less than one year old, leaving his mother with a small boy to bring up alone. With no money coming in, "Miss Hettie" opened up her house, renting an apartment and rooms to many of the teachers at the local school. She also worked at the school cafeteria for years, fondly acquiring the nickname "Cook." She was very active at the Baptist church, even though she was brought up before the church for square dancing during her younger years. Since Miss Hettie played the piano at church, young Bill never missed a funeral.

Bill remembers when the mill burned down one night. It was located across the road from where they lived, and the wind was blowing toward the house. They were afraid that the sparks would set the roof of the house on fire, so the neighbors helped Miss Hettie soak blankets and quilts in water and spread them on the roof. It worked quite well; the house is still there after almost ninety years.

Many members of Miss Hettie's family worked for the railroad; in fact, Bill can still recite the train schedule through Summerfield: 11:21 a.m. and 5:14 p.m. He also recalls their unique system of getting messages to a family member on the train: Bill and some of the other boys would wad up paper and set it on fire on the railroad track. The train would then have to stop, giving them enough time to pass along the message.

After all these years, Bill still remembers one special night when he witnessed some unexpected excitement at the depot. While he was there, several strange cars pulled up and men got out carrying guns. These G-men had heard that a robber was onboard the train. An excited eight-year-old Billy was there when they found the robber hiding between the boxcars!

He and other Summerfield teenagers loved baseball and would hobo the train to Greensboro to attend games. He doesn't remember how they got home; they must have hitchhiked because there was no late train.

Bill graduated from high school at age fifteen and attended Appalachian State College for one year. The next two years he worked at Reich Funeral Home in Greensboro. He recalls being on ambulance duty the night C.L. "Syke" Scarlette had an accident at the garage and ended up losing his leg. Dr. C.H. Fryar was riding with them in the ambulance taking Syke to the hospital. The driver was going so fast that Dr. Fryar told the teenage Bill, "Just let me out; I can't take this." Bill then warned the driver, "Slow down. If you don't, we're going to lose Doc; he's going to have a heart attack!"

At age nineteen, Bill decided to enter Wake Forest University. During his tenure at Wake Forest, he stayed home one semester and worked for Joe Vaughn at his funeral home and grocery store in Stokesdale. After graduating from Wake Forest, Bill became part of the first four-year class to graduate from Bowman-Gray Medical School in Winston-Salem. He then interned at North Carolina Baptist Hospital. Soon afterward he volunteered for World War II, spending a year in the Pacific theatre.

When he was in high school, Bill became well known for singing at most of the school functions. He also sang at the radio station located in the O'Henry Hotel in Greensboro. The Soil Conservation Corps paid Bill to sing and Margaret Medearis Metz to accompany him on the piano. They even sent a truck from Greensboro to pick them up and deliver them back home.

While Bill was in medical school, he helped pay his expenses by serving as a paid tenor soloist at churches in Winston-Salem and Raleigh. He was a featured soloist at the governor's mansion from 1938 through 1941.

Dr. William "Bill" Shields and his wife, Arlene. *Courtesy Suzanne Shields King.*

He appeared as soloist with the North Carolina and Winston-Salem symphony orchestras and sang for many other organizations, as well as on radio and television.

He studied music for fourteen years under Lorne Grant, a graduate of Julliard School of Music. Finally, Mr. Grant told Bill that he'd have to make a decision. Did he want to major in music or medicine? Bill chose medicine but also indulged his love of music with volunteer singing throughout the country as a featured soloist and by directing church choirs.

Bill practiced medicine in Summerfield, Stokesdale and Reidsville before moving to Texas. When he had an office in Stokesdale, if he and Arlene, his wife, wanted to go anywhere at night, they had to meet somewhere other than at home. The reason? There were always patients waiting at their house in Summerfield to see him. The patients didn't see the logic of driving all the way to Stokesdale to see the doctor when they could simply drive down the street.

After moving to Texas, Bill became a surgeon and was chief of surgical services at Wadley Hospital in Texarkana. Although busy with his medical career, he and his wife have traveled worldwide, sometimes on mission trips. There are very few countries they've missed. He also traveled while he was in military service and with the Central Intelligence Agency doing "undercover" work. His family now includes four children, four grandchildren and one great-grandchild—plus a cat and a dog.

Although he left Summerfield for greener pastures in Texas, part of his heart remains in Summerfield. He and his wife came back a few years ago for a visit and, as he put it, "loved seeing all the landmarks from my childhood as well as all the wonderful new changes."

Thanks to Bill, Arlene and their daughter Suzanne for sharing their memories.

HE MAKES WOOD COME TO LIFE

Our national symbol is the eagle, and around the Fourth of July we usually think more about the flag and other patriotic symbols. Buddy Isley does more than just think about them. He didn't set out to carve an eagle like the national symbol. His interpretation is an eagle at rest with its head tucked down; he calls it *Peace*. A few years ago, the eagle and some of his other woodcarvings were on display at the Greensboro Public Library.

His bust of George Washington is carved from walnut; Buddy estimates the wood to be at least one hundred years old. He says that the old wood doesn't crack when carved, which sometimes happens with newer wood. He used redwood for the bust of Abraham Lincoln.

Watching his father work with wood might have influenced Buddy to take up carving. His dad was a carpenter, and once he needed a rounded piece of wood for a project. After soaking the wood for a few days, he

Buddy Isley with some of his woodcarvings. *Courtesy the author.*

tied it between some trees to form the shape he wanted and let it dry. It worked perfectly for his project. Buddy followed in his father's footsteps and worked as a carpenter for many years.

Perhaps carving soap at school influenced his decision as well, but whatever the reason, he decided to try carving wood several years ago. He's never had a lesson and just looks at the wood to get an idea of what to carve. Sometimes he says he just gets a feeling of what the wood should be. He always tries to incorporate the grain of the wood into his carving.

One of his first projects was to make a wooden scrapbook cover for the Woman's Missionary Union at Summerfield First Baptist Church, at the request of Marietta Thore. He carved the initials WMU and several WMU symbols on the cover. The scrapbook now holds a place of honor in the Heritage Room of the church.

He enjoys hunting rocks and gems and polishing the stones, athough he hasn't gotten into jewelry making with the stones and gems he finds.

He has a small collection of arrowheads and other American Indian artifacts he has found.

History, especially Summerfield history, also brings him much pleasure. He's had a history exhibit at every Founder's Day event since the first one in 1996. An old adding machine, which was used in the Brittain Store in earlier days, was rescued by Buddy and is now displayed in the Summerfield Town Hall. He also found several old small bottles near the town hall which are now in the museum there.

His collection of tools includes a lot of small chisels and many different types and sizes of knives. He needs all of them to carve tiny details, such as hair and feathers. He uses the knots in the wood or natural cracks or other imperfections to enhance the carving. On a walking stick, a knot became the nose and mouth of a bear. He uses no stains on the wood, just sealer so the natural color of the wood can be seen.

Wherever he goes, Buddy keeps an eye out for wood he can use. One day while doing some work on Jack Claybrook's house, he saw a rather small walnut tree that had died. He told Jack that he'd like to have a piece of the wood, and Jack said, "Take the whole tree." When they were taking up the railroad tracks through Summerfield, Buddy asked for some railroad ties. He used part of one of the ties, probably over one hundred years old, to carve the head of a Native American. The feather is carved from the same piece of wood rather than carved separately and attached.

Another one of his projects was located in the children's department of First Baptist Church. When Marietta Thore was the leader of Mission Friends, she asked Buddy if he could build a small church that the children could play in. He built one complete with a small steeple, and the children enjoyed taking their chairs and dolls and sitting inside the little church.

His woodcarvings and other projects give pleasure to many people, young and old alike.

AN EARLY SUMMERFIELD ENTREPRENEUR

William H. Brittain apparently had an interest in many different types of business. William, one of the sons of Joseph Brittain, died in July 1865, leaving a wife and five small children.

William's first wife was Sarah Saunders, daughter of Hezekiah and Rebecca Saunders. Hezekiah built and operated Saunders Inn. After Sarah's death, William married Catherine Ogburn, daughter of Edmund Ogburn and Jane Lanier Ogburn.

Mr. Brittain probably started out as a farmer, but by April 1853 he was advertising his country store at Summerfield or Bruce's Crossroads. He had just returned from a trip to New York and Philadelphia, where he had purchased a large stock of plain and fancy dry goods, groceries, hardware, cutlery and agricultural implements. His advertisement stated that he would exchange goods for all kinds of country produce and allow fair prices. It's not known how long he operated the store.

In 1839, he was the owner of a thoroughbred horse, Nick Biddle, sired by Fylde, who had won the Chester Cup in 1828. Fylde was imported from England to Virginia in 1832 but was crippled in the landing from the ship. How Mr. Brittain became the owner of Nick Biddle is unknown, but the horse evidently didn't become a famous racehorse.

Brittain's Hotel, sometimes called the Brittain House, formerly the Bland House in Greensboro, opened for business on May 18, 1857. William H. Brittain was the proprietor and advertised pleasantly furnished rooms and a well-served table. Travelers were assured that "horseflesh shall not suffer in his stables for want of provender or attention." It was said that Confederate paroles were issued there.

At least one traveler didn't have anything complimentary to say about the Brittain House. In an article in the July 18, 1865 edition of the *Philadelphia Enquirer*, the writer criticized the "dumpy, two-story affair," stating that the brick columns had lost much of their plastering and the planks of the porch floor had rotted ends. He also criticized the food and said that if the butter was old you could ask for a glass of buttermilk and scoop out enough butter for your bread. As this was only a few months after the end of the Civil War, it would seem that he expected too much!

According to some notes written by Clyde Smith, the railroad was being built during the operation of the Brittain Hotel, and some of the railroad men stayed there. When the railroad from Greensboro to Salisbury was completed, Catherine Brittain was an honorary guest on the first trip on the new railroad. Mr. Smith also stated that both the farm and the hotel were operated with slave labor.

At the time of his death, Mr. Brittain owned stock in the North Carolina Central Railroad, a Guilford County bond, a lot on the Plank Road in

High Point and 640 acres in Bosque County, Texas, in addition to the hotel and two farms in Summerfield.

William and Catherine's daughter, Sallie, married John R. Smith. The Smiths built a house on Oak Ridge Road near the Saunders Inn. The house was later used as Lynch's Lodge, according to Margaret Metz. Henry Clay Brittain, son of William and Catherine, didn't operate a hotel, but he was a farmer and operated a country store like his father.

PART II

Places

Stafford Store Building Has Colorful History

The Stafford Brothers Store was opened in May 1922 and was owned and operated by Buck and Lee Stafford. It was located next to the feed mill on Summerfield Road.

In November 1926, robbers were caught red-handed inside the store. Frank West and Jack Hardin, who said they were from Lynchburg, Virginia, broke through a window of the store. Someone heard the noise, and Lee Stafford, Jim Proctor and others surrounded the store. The robbers had piled up a large quantity of merchandise and were getting ready to make a fast getaway when Lee Stafford opened the front door and called on them to surrender. Sheriff D.B. Stafford was called, and the two young men were carried to jail.

Less than a year later, the store was robbed again, this time about 1:30 a.m. A family living across the road from the store told officers the next day that someone in the family saw a touring car drive up and stop in front of the store. The people in the car threw out some tools, and the family assumed that a tire was being repaired, so they thought no more about it.

Apparently, it was the next morning when one or both of the Stafford brothers went to open the store that the robbery was discovered. A nearby blacksmith shop had been broken into and tools taken to use in the store robbery.

The front door of the store had been forced open. The door to the safe in the store was unlocked, and using the stolen tools, the robbers had forced open the inner door of the safe and had taken about seventy-five dollars from the money drawer. Some merchandise was also taken and hauled away in the car. No clear fingerprints could be found; the only trace left by the robbers was some tire tracks.

Bea Stafford Curtis, daughter of Lee Stafford, remembers her daddy giving her candy when she went to see him at the store. The Stafford brothers also owned the mill next door to the store and the blacksmith shop across the road. They had ice for sale, and Bea thought they kept the ice from melting by storing it in the sawdust piles nearby.

Bea and her brother, Bob, played around the store most every day. When they swept the floor of the store, bottle caps were swept out into the yard. One day, when Bea and Bob were playing in the yard, Bob found a nickel among the bottle caps. Bea had been going to the cottage prayer meetings in the community with her mother, so she started praying "Lord, help me find a nickel" over and over. But she didn't find a nickel—she found a dime! Bea said her faith really increased that day.

After the Staffords stopped using the building as a store, it was used for other purposes. Stafford Powder was made there, probably during the Depression, according to Bea. The powder was a foot and body deodorant, probably only made for a short period of time.

The building was also used as a cough drop factory by Smith Brothers probably in 1939 or 1940–41. A newspaper item in January 1942 mentions "the Smith Brothers old factory." Jimmy Harrell remembered that the cough drop factory closed up and left with no notice. David and Clyde Robinson Jr. also remember the factory, and Clyde thinks part of the sign said "Cough Drops." Dewey Trogdon remembers that there was a sign on the front of the building saying "Smith Bros." (Maybe it read "Smith Bros. Cough Drops.") Dewey also remembers huge kettles on legs inside the building. They left lots of big five-gallon or larger glass jugs outside the building.

After the Negro school burned in 1942, the store building was used as a school until a new school building was finished. Daphne Curtis Fitzgerald remembers that they had no benches or chairs so they sat on boards placed on bricks.

Sometime before January 1940, probably 1937 or 1938, Jim Belton used the building for a small grocery store/pool hall for an unknown length of time. (Ruffin Case died in January 1940, and since he's in the

Grocery store/pool hall run by Jim Belton in the Stafford Store Building about 1937 or 1938. *Left to right*: Jim Belton, Jay Winfree, Earl Turner, Aubrey Holt, Paul Murphy and Ruffin Case. *Courtesy Mike Belton.*

photo it had to be before that date.) The building is still there, and for many years it has been used as a residence.

Thanks to all who shared their memories and to Mike Belton for sharing the photo and for taking the time to visit Paul Murphy, before his death, and getting his help to identify the people in the photo.

Rest Homes Were Part of Community Life

Stokesdale has Countryside Manor, a nursing home that was opened in 1977 by Dr. Mervin and Virginia King and Sonny and Phyllis Harris. Although Summerfield never had a nursing home, we did have at least three rest homes.

The first was Hood's Rest Home, operated by Myrtle and Herman Hood. It was located on Summerfield Road, where the mobile home park is now located, and was in the C.O. Martin House. The date it was opened is unknown, but it was in operation in 1958. Mrs. Dora Parrish Capps died there on April 27, 1958.

While Hood's Rest Home was still in operation, Mrs. Elsie Friddle opened a rest home in her house on Oak Ridge Road. She only had a license for four residents, and they were treated like members of the family. Mrs. Friddle was known for her good cooking; Buddy Isley remembers her fried apple pies stacked high on a platter. Sarah Friddle remembers her delicious vegetable soup and yeast rolls. Jean Friddle Isley remembers that Ollie Gourley, a resident, said that Mrs. Friddle could take almost nothing and come up with the best meal she'd ever tasted.

Jean also said that her mother, Mrs. Friddle, always had a big garden and canned lots of vegetables for the winter. The residents helped to string green beans and shell lima beans. Cleo Purvis, one of the residents, sometimes helped Mrs. Friddle carry the jars of vegetables to the basement for storage. One day she remarked, "Seeing all the canned goods in the basement is like walking into Winn-Dixie."

Some of the other residents Jean remembers were Lola Peeden, Mrs. Steele, Esther Stewart, Emma Lloyd, Mrs. Hancock and Patsy Bodenheimer.

Mrs. Friddle came up with an unusual way for the residents to get their exercise. Herbert Scarlette remembered seeing Mrs. Friddle walking with the residents from her house to the crossroads and then back home. It wasn't such a long walk, and there wasn't much traffic on Oak Ridge Road then.

It must have been after the Hoods gave up the operation of their rest home that Mrs. Ruby Winfree took over in the Martin house on Summerfield Road. She continued operating a rest home in the house after it was moved across Highway 220.

Sunday school classes and other groups from the Baptist church, and perhaps from other churches, visited the residents at all three rest homes. Once when a class carried refreshments for a party for the residents, one of the ladies said that she'd never been to a party before. The Young People's Training Union group presented a simple Christmas program for the residents one year.

The Baptist church had an outreach Sunday school class in the rest home after the house was moved across Highway 220. Dianna Scarlette was the teacher and Frances Nelson was the secretary. They held the class during the regular Sunday school hour, and then Dianna and Frances went to the worship service at the church.

Various groups or individuals would go almost every Sunday to sing, and the ladies really enjoyed the special singing. For several years, Mary

Junior Girls Class from First Baptist Church visit Winfree's Rest Home in 1969. *Seated, left to right*: Kathy Gravely; a resident of the home; Carol Huffman; and Sharon Spencer. *Standing, left to right*: unidentified; Melody Shelton; a resident; Ruby Winfree, owner/operator of the home; a resident; possibly Debra Doggett; and Teresa Osborne. *Courtesy the author.*

Ruth Fryar and I carried books from the church library every two weeks for the ladies to read.

Sometimes when the GAs (or Girls in Action, a mission group at the Baptist church) went to visit Winfree's Rest Home, they sang Christmas carols and took candy for the residents. There were two age groups; some of the girls were very young, and Bonnie Thore Pitts remembers being a little afraid of going to talk to the ladies and singing for them. One of the ladies enjoyed their singing so much that she had an unusual request for them; she wanted them to sing at her funeral. Bonnie remembers that she and her sister Darlene and Gloria Patterson honored her request and sang at the funeral.

BEAUTY SHOP OF THE PAST WAS FOUND IN HOME

Years ago, before Great Clips, Leon's and so many other beauty salons came on the scene, people had shops in their homes. One of the earliest home beauty shops in Summerfield was opened by Helen Ayers in 1936.

At one time it was located upstairs in the Ayers's brick home, near the present town hall. I remember being in her shop one time; she was shampooing someone's hair and the water stopped running. She went to the door and yelled downstairs, "Cut the water off; I can't get any water up here!"

Lots of people remember going to Helen's shop but don't remember the name of it. Summerfield Beauty Shop was advertised in the 1948 school annual. That could have been Helen's because her shop closed in 1950.

Ruby Price had a shop in her house; Ruby did Frances Belton Angel's hair when she got married in November 1938. Polly Hendrick Irby remembers getting a perm there about 1947. After a few years, Ruby closed her shop and started selling Stanley products.

Some of the other people who had shops in their homes included Lib Angel, whose shop opened about 1961. It was appropriately named Lib's Beauty Shop. Advertised in the 1962 school annual were Jones Beauty Shop and Anna Lou's Beauty Shop, operated by Anna Lou Preston. Fentress Beauty Salon was opened about 1961 by Izula Fentress. Others who had shops were Maedell Norman, Florence Stafford Westmoreland, Sheila Key, Barbara Heath and Sue Atkins.

Novella Watkins remembers that Esther Ogburn in Summerfield and Pauline Crutchfield and Pearl Watkins in Oak Ridge were some of the black ladies who had shops in their homes.

When Billie Lou Everett was a little girl, she and her cousins played beauty shop when they went to visit their Grandpa Smothers. They finger waved one another's hair using sugar water. Both Sybil Neal and Billie Lou grew up and became beauticians. Billie Lou also taught cosmetology for fifteen years at Guilford Technical Community College (GTCC).

A shampoo and set was fifty cents when Billie Lou opened her shop in 1949. She had customers from Oak Ridge to Stokesdale to Brown Summit. One day she did ten perms—a grand total of fifty dollars!

Sometimes while Bea Stafford Curtis was sitting under the dryer, she'd give Billie Lou's small daughter, Mary Lou, her bottle. Thelma Bray

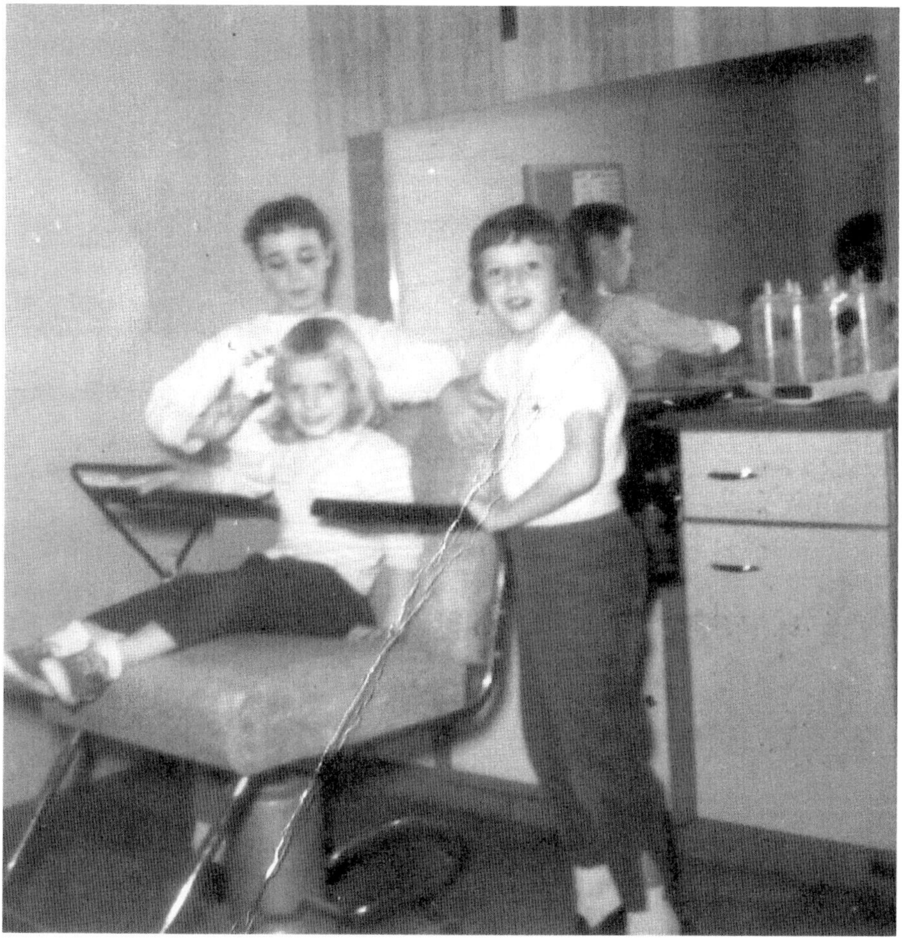

Billie Lou's Beauty Shop about 1960. *Standing, left to right*: Jane Morton (Hohn) and Patsy Morton (Long). *Seated*: Mary Lou Morton (Mooney). *Courtesy Billie Lou Morton.*

sometimes came at 6:00 a.m. for a shampoo and set before she went to work at 8:00 a.m. Billie Lou fixed some breakfast for Thelma to eat while her hair dried.

Some, if not all, of these beauticians went the "extra mile" for their customers. Billie Lou remembers going to customers' homes, the nursing home or even the funeral home to do their hair. Dianna Scarlette remembered Lib Angel doing a shampoo and set for free if there was a death in the customer's family.

Even though the men didn't get shampoos and sets, they had to have their hair cut. In the 1930s, Charlie Everett would go to the Old Brick Store, now called Hillsdale Brick Store, on Saturday afternoon to operate a "barbershop" on the porch. He carried his hand clippers, scissors and a cloth to put around their necks; and with a straight chair from the store, he was ready for business! Wouldn't it be interesting to know what he charged.

Charlie "Ed" Warren in Oak Ridge and Jim Hall and Zebedee Frazier in Stokesdale were black barbers who Novella Watkins remembers having barbershops in their homes.

Ira Johnson had a barbershop over Brittain's Store in 1911. Dura Mae Ayers remembered that in 1938 Edward Combs had a barbershop, and his wife, Catherine, had a beauty shop in the back of the Brittain Store. Dura Mae also remembered that Helen Ayers had a shop there at one time. Reverend Settlemyre was said to have operated a barbershop there before Mr. Combs, and Walter Rice is thought to have had a shop there at some time.

Gladys Murphy remembered that her father, "Sam" Case, had a barbershop at the side of Ellington's Store. Mr. Kirby, "Pick" Kirby and Kenny Price had a barbershop in the Winfree Shopping Center.

Ernest Fletcher had a shop at the back of the old garage on Summerfield Road, next to Tuttle's Supermarket. He not only cut hair but offered shaves, and in earlier years, before many people had indoor bathrooms, Dewey Trogdon said that you could get a shower there for fifteen cents. Dewey said that he and "Jack" Winfree shared a shower once. Now that was a cheap shower! But a dunking in the schoolhouse lake was even cheaper. Dewey said they always liked to use Ivory soap in the lake because it floated in the water.

Things have changed a lot over the years; now home beauty shops and barbershops are mostly a thing of the past.

Thanks to all those mentioned and to Linda Southard, Barbara Trogdon, Ruth Chambers, Bob Brittain, Robert Morton, Alma Tilley and Hilda Pegram for sharing their memories.

CASE'S STORE FONDLY REMEMBERED BY MANY

Several things about Case's Store are uncertain, such as when the store was built and when T.E. "Ed" Case started operating the store. Herbert Scarlette remembered hearing that the store was formerly a livery stable,

Case's Store building about 1948, operated at that time by Austin and Andrew Tuttle. *Courtesy Norma and Austin Tuttle.*

and when it was made into a store, a floor had to be put into the building. It could have been the livery stable run by Hill and Miles in 1912. Their livery stable was located near the depot, and they advertised that they would carry passengers anywhere they wanted to go.

T.E. Case and his wife, Dexie, were running the store by 1930 and perhaps earlier. Helen Jones Angel remembers Mrs. Case helping in the store. Jimmy Harrell remembered the ladder that was used to reach items on the top shelves; it was set on rollers and could be moved where it was needed. Zeb Jones remembers Oren Lloyd, who worked in the store for many years, sometimes using a long pole with a hook on the end to reach items on high shelves. Dewey Trogdon remembers delivering groceries for Mr. Case to Miss Fanny Davis, Mrs. Lee Stafford and Miss Callie Allred. The pay was sweet; Mr. Case paid off in Mr. Goodbars and Hershey bars.

"Jackie" Pegram remembers her third-grade teacher allowing the girls to go to Case's Store to spend their pennies. There were always three girls in her group; they had to go down the back street instead of the main highway. They loved the suckers and BB Bats. One day they wanted some kind of candy and didn't have quite enough money for it, but Mr. Case let them have it anyway.

Mary Alice Wilson Pope remembers her Uncle Ed giving her suckers when she went to the store. The Cases didn't have any children. Mary

Frances Case Russell remembers going to the store with her mother. She well remembers Mrs. Case saying to her mother, "You have all these children; why don't you give me one?" Maybe Mary Frances was afraid that her mother might decide to give her away!

In May 1932, there was a lot of excitement at the store. Thieves entered the store one Tuesday night and took more than one hundred dollars' worth of merchandise. Some of the stolen goods were found and carried to the sheriff's office before the robbery was even reported! The robbers carried off at least thirty pairs of overalls; they also took pants, shirts, women's hose, men's socks, shoes, cigars, cigarettes, flashlights, an electric clock and other articles. They were unsuccessful in their attempts to force open the safe, which was thought to contain a large sum of money.

Less exciting but of much interest was the beautiful quilt displayed in the store window in April 1941. It was called a stamp quilt, because it had so many small pieces, and Mrs. Case offered a prize to the person guessing the number of pieces in the quilt.

Carol Byrd Sellars was a great-niece of the Cases and remembers the potbellied stove and the pickle barrel, but her favorite memory is dancing for the customers when she visited the store as a little girl.

The Cases were still operating the store in March 1946. Sometime between then and 1948, the Tuttle twins, Andrew and Austin, took over the operation of the store. Gary Long remembers helping them in the store; they sold oilcloth, had wire baskets of eggs and ground coffee for customers while they waited.

Andrew Tuttle was killed in an auto accident in October 1948, but Austin continued running the store. About 1953 or 1954, Austin and his wife, Norma, built a new brick store next to the old white frame building, which was later torn down. Tuttle's Super Market was the first modern supermarket in Summerfield. Gary Long also worked there after school, putting up stock and bagging groceries for two or three dollars per week. Sometimes Austin would sneak off, and he and Gary would fly around all afternoon in Austin's small plane. Needless to say, that didn't make Norma too happy.

After the store was broken into several times, Norma started taking the money home each night—in a cigar box! She put the box in a grocery bag and put groceries on top of the box.

In 1982, Gary Long bought the store and operated it for ten years; at one time he had fifteen employees. Irene Clodfelter worked at the cash register for many years. The building is still there but now is home to Full

Gospel Tabernacle Church. The building that started out as a place to dispense groceries now dispenses spiritual sustenance.

In addition to those mentioned, thanks to Karen Tuttle McCanless and Jane Tuttle, two of the daughters of Norma and Austin Tuttle, for sharing their memories.

Granite Gym Is a Grand Old Gem

The Summerfield gym is a real gem. It was completed by September 29, 1939. In the beginning, it was called the Summerfield recreation park, and plans included a lake, bathhouses and a community clubhouse.

This was one of the WPA projects in Guilford County; another was the gym at Allen Jay School. Though WPA stands for Works Project Administration, some of the locals said it stood for We Poke Along. The county commissioners voted in July 1934 to purchase 63.2 acres of land from Charles H. Willson and Joseph A. Hoskins at a cost of $2,600.

Part of the cost for the project came from WPA funds, but the community was responsible for about 30 percent of the total cost. The community was allowed to furnish labor and material instead of all cash. Even the schoolchildren helped by bringing tobacco to be sold and by selling plants donated by Mrs. Joe Trescher.

In a contest among the grades for raising gymnasium funds during the last week of October 1938, Miss Placid Bennett's fifth-grade class contributed twelve pounds of tobacco, $6.10 in cash and $3.80 from the sale of flowers. The eighth-grade class of Miss Mary Pinnix came in second with eleven pounds of tobacco, $6.15 in cash and $0.50 from flowers. The entire proceeds from the Halloween Carnival in 1939—$114.43—was to be used to purchase a heating system for the new gym.

Frances Smith Long, Robert Morton and Dr. "Bill" Shields all remember the potbellied stoves in the gym. There was a stove at each end, enclosed by railings for the safety of the basketball players. Robert also remembers a railing in front of the bleachers. Were the stoves bought with the proceeds from the Halloween Carnival?

By December 1938, the stonework on the gym's west and north sides was completed, and the stonework on the dam for the lake was almost completed. Dewey Trogdon remembers his father telling him

The granite gym at Summerfield High School was completed in 1939 by the WPA and is still used by Summerfield Elementary School. *Courtesy Bill Gordon.*

that the rock for the gym came from the "Bob" Gamble farm on Pleasant Ridge Road.

Bill Gordon said that his brother, Bob, was in the first grade and remembers seeing his father's truck going by the school hauling rock for the gym; he thinks that Howard Pope was driving. Mildred Pope Jessup remembers her father, Howard Pope, talking about hauling rock. He and O.C. Wall, both of whom worked for R.C. Gordon, chiseled some of the rock for the gym. I wonder how many Summerfield men helped chisel those rocks.

When the gym was almost finished, Clyde Robinson Jr. remembers asking for permission to get some of the scrap lumber. He hauled the scraps home with his pony and wagon. Then he made rabbit gums from the scraps and set some of the gums as far away as Reedy Fork Creek. He skinned the rabbits and sold them to railroad personnel for one dollar each. His father told him, "Leave the heads on so the men will know they're not cats!"

September 29, 1939, was a big day in Summerfield. The handsome granite gymnasium and community center was dedicated with all seats filled and many people standing. The structure was accepted on behalf of Guilford County by R. Flake Shaw, a county commissioner and Summerfield farmer. Many important people were there from other parts of the state.

Lee A. Stafford, chairman of the ticket committee, said that over 2,000 people were expected. J.G. Long supervised the preparation of the barbecue and Brunswick stew. W.B. Stafford secured Tal Henry and his orchestra to provide music for dancing in the new gym. Between 1,000 and 1,500 people were in attendance. There must have been a lot of tired but happy people when the festivities were over.

Many basketball games and other community events have taken place since the gym was dedicated in 1939. School reunions have been held in the gym. It was used during the first Summerfield Founders Day and has been used many times over the years for people to cast their votes during elections.

During the 2009 Founders Day celebration, a sock hop organized by Bill and Mary Jane Gordon was held at the gym. On Founders Day, the gym was open for people to look around and reminisce about basketball games and other events in the past.

When the gym was built, it was for the Summerfield High School, but the high school building was torn down in 1983. It was replaced with Summerfield Elementary School, and the gym still rings with the shouts of boys and girls at play. Delane Williams said that three generations of her family had played ball in the gym; she, her father and now her son. Hopefully, this grand old gym will be the scene of many more basketball games and numerous other happy events for years to come.

PART III

Events

Christmas at Ridgefield School, 1885

During his senior year at Oak Ridge Institute, T.E. Whitaker was asked to teach at Ridgefield School. He needed the extra money, and the school term only lasted three months—four weeks before Christmas and eight weeks after Christmas.

For a young man still in school himself, this was quite an undertaking, even though he was paid twenty-five dollars per month. The school was a log cabin with a dirt floor, and most of the chinking was gone from between the logs. The door squeaked on wooden hinges. Thirty-four students with almost no books sounds like an impossible task. Most of the textbooks had come down from former generations; some were so old that they contained the old-style "s" that looked like an "f" in print. With the exception of Webster's Blue Back Speller, no two books were alike.

Whitaker's students were Bob, Will and Dave Stafford; Martha, Will and Clint Stanley; Sallie, Belle and Nannie Booker; Star, Ed and Charlie Higgins; Jesse and Jim Bull; Bud and Martin Highfill; John and Charlie Stuart; Elva and Sallie McKaughan; Allen, Oscar and Jasper Peedin; Walter and Fanny Nelson; Bud and Mollie Huffines; Matt, Will and Vanny Rayle; Will Crutchfield; Tom and Delaney Peek; Tom, Ida and Mattie Knight; and Minnie Hunt. Dave Stafford, mentioned above, later became the sheriff of Guilford County.

The teacher boarded about a mile and a half from the school and started on his walk to school before the sun was up. He only missed one day of school, when the water in the creek was too high to cross. The school day didn't end until every child had had his lesson. There were no desks; the children sat on backless benches made of slabs with pegs for legs. The only "writing desk" was a smooth plank bracketed to the wall.

There was a big fireplace at one end of the building, and the older students had to go out in the nearby woods and get dead trees to burn. There was a stove at the other end of the building. Even with a fire at both ends, the children were probably still cold.

Ridgefield School was located near where Pleasant Ridge Church now stands. John Stafford, the grandfather of Sheriff David Stafford, gave the land for the first schoolhouse at Ridgefield. Some of the teachers who preceded Mr. Whitaker were Charles Case, John C. Bunch, Albert Clark, Peel Robinson (somewhat illegible in source), Joel Wilson, Clay Brittain, Martin McMichael, Jesse Stanley, Mrs. P.N. Hall, Mrs. Fanny Ross, Parthenia Henley, Mary Kirkman, Mollie Owens and J.C. Lasley.

On the morning before the Christmas holidays, when the teacher arrived at school, he found the door barred! He could hear the children whispering and laughing. When he demanded entrance, there was a loud protest from inside. He pretended great wrath and threatened dire punishment if the door was not opened at once.

He was familiar with the custom of "locking the teacher out" until a treat was promised. He had come prepared with a bucket of store candy, which he had hidden in the woods. After promising the children their treat, the door was promptly opened, and Whitaker sent some of the students to fetch the candy. The children had to wait impatiently until noon for their treat.

Two young men came by about noon with their banjos, and after the candy was distributed, they furnished music for outdoor games. One of the parents later complained that the teacher had allowed banjo picking and dancing on the school grounds. Mr. Whitaker was sure that he was going to be fired, but when the school committeemen visited the school and listened to the children spell, read and recite, the complaint against him wasn't even mentioned, much to his relief.

At the end of the school term, public examinations were held during the day, but the program that night was given over to indoor games. Some of the games they played were "Drop the Handkerchief" and "King William was King George's Son," with the teacher also taking part. Music furnished by two banjos and a fiddle was the highlight of the evening. There was even a young couple from Oak Ridge there on their honeymoon!

Even though the children enjoyed the end of school entertainment, "locking the teacher out" and the Christmas treats were probably their favorite school memories.

Angel Donated Land for Baptist Church

Summerfield Baptist Church, now First Baptist, was constituted in July 1860 with eighteen members from Elm Grove Baptist Church near Stokesdale. Those charter members were Henry Barbee, Nancy Barbee, Bettie Baynes, J.M. Baynes, Martha Baynes, C. Case, Hannah Case, Jane Johnson, Lucinda Lock, Cynthia P. Powell, S.A. Powell, Abigail Saunders, Isabella Jane Stevens, Mary Stevens, Catherine Willson, Rebecca Willson, Thomas Willson and W.C. Winfrey. Descendants of some of the charter members are still members of the church today.

One of the charter members, Abigail Saunders, is believed to be the wife of Hezekiah Saunders, or Sanders, who owned and operated Saunders Inn, also known as the Travelers Inn. Margaret Metz enjoyed telling about "Aunt Abbie" making her clothes to be buried in, as most older people did then.

Aunt Abbie, Mrs. Metz said, made a black silk dress but got carried away when she started making her petticoats. She had seven cotton petticoats all stiffly starched and ironed. When the time came to prepare her for burial, all the petticoats wouldn't fit in the coffin, so they had to take off three of them. Mrs. Metz laughed and said, "Poor Aunt Abbie had to meet her maker in disgrace with only four petticoats!"

For many years, any religious group was allowed to meet in the old Brick School, built in the 1830s. The Baptists met there before they had a building and sometimes in the Summerfield Academy and Business Institute building. In 1870, there was talk of a committee to confer with the Methodists about building a joint house of worship, but apparently that idea didn't get past the talking stage.

The pine tree planted before 1914 by T. Milton Angel in front of First Baptist Church of Summerfield. *Courtesy the author.*

How many churches can say that the land for their building was given by an Angel? When the Baptists started talking again in 1884 about a building, T. Milton Angel agreed to donate one acre of land for the project. The church accepted the gift and bought an additional acre for fifteen dollars.

Milton Angel planted a longleaf pine tree near the church, which is now directly in front of the sanctuary. It's not known just when he planted the tree, but he died in 1914, so it's probably about one hundred years old.

The church's "ghost tale" also involved Mr. Angel. His son Benjamin spoke later in life about sitting on the steps one evening about 1902 and looking toward the church nearby. He noticed a light in the church cemetery; the light was moving slowly among the graves. Ben thought that it might be someone with a lantern, but as he continued to watch, the light moved around the side of the church toward the front. Suddenly, it shot straight up in the air, circled the church steeple twice and disappeared!

Carfey Doggett was baptized about 1924 or 1925 at Ogburn's pond. Tom Moore was baptized at the same time, but the preacher ran into a bit of a problem. Carfey said that when the preacher dipped Mr. Moore's head underwater, his feet came up, and when the preacher pushed his feet under, his head came up. He tried several times and never could get all of Mr. Moore underwater at the same time. Finally, the preacher said, "Well, it's all right, he's wet from head to toe!"

The first organ at the church caused quite a controversy. Carfey Doggett remembers his dad telling the story. Some men from Connecticut and New York came down to Summerfield every year to go hunting. They stayed in a log cabin on the Doggett property.

One fall, the hunters, some Republicans and some Democrats, were here at election time. Two of the men wagered on the presidential election. They decided that the winner would give $100 for an organ to the Baptist church, where the Doggetts were members. After the election, the men tried to give the money to the church, and the controversy was on.

There must have been many heated discussions about the pros and cons of accepting money from a wager for an organ. Everybody in the community probably voiced their opinion on the matter, whether or not they were members of the church. Finally, after several months of discussion, the church members agreed to accept the money. They sent a resolution of thanks to J.T. Davies and E.L. Rapalla of New York, and a copy of the resolution was also sent to the *Biblical Recorder*, the state Baptist paper.

I wonder if hearing that organ played always stirred up some unpleasant memories for some members of the church.

Christmas Programs of Old

Like most everything else, church Christmas programs have changed over the years. Many years ago, according to Margaret Metz, most people in Summerfield didn't have Christmas trees at home. The Methodist and Baptist churches had trees, and they used real candles on them; the candles were lit during the Christmas program.

Dura Mae Ayers wondered why the trees didn't catch fire. Margaret Metz said the tree at the Methodist church actually caught on fire one year. Thanks to the foresight of someone in the church, a tragedy was prevented—there was always a bucket of water near the tree for just such

Christmas tree at Stokesdale United Methodist Church, circa 1940s or early 1950s. *Courtesy Pauline Robinson.*

an emergency. Back then the churches probably didn't have expensive carpeting, and the wooden floor would soon dry.

The trees were always cedars cut by some of the men in the church. At the Baptist church, "Jap" Angel provided the tree for years and also gathered bunches of "running cedar," as we called it. Sometimes bricks with holes in them were put in the windows. Candles were placed in the holes, and the bricks were covered with "running cedar." People sitting near the windows kept an eye on the candles. The church smelled so good as the scent of cedar filled the air.

I don't remember candles on the trees, but we didn't have electric lights on the trees for years. I remember the colored glass balls and foil icicles. The tree was always a big one and reached almost to the ceiling—and our church had a high ceiling. Our tree must have looked like the one at Stokesdale Methodist Church.

One of my favorite parts of the Christmas program was the recitations by the smaller children. Sometimes they only said a few words or a few lines, but it was their chance to be a star. Even if the lines weren't humorous, Martha Robinson and Judy Hohn usually managed to do something to get everybody to laugh. After the recitations, the children usually knelt around the manger and sang "Away in a Manger."

The Christmas story was always acted out, with Mary and Joseph, the shepherds (in bathrobes with towels on their heads) and the Wise Men. Some of the men cut down small trees and bent one end to form the shepherd's crook; sometimes twine was wrapped around the crook to hold it in place. Our church never used a real baby as Jesus, and I don't think a doll was ever used.

At times, the role of the angel was a hard job—even though the angel usually didn't have a speaking part. Linda Southard remembers her mother being the angel one year and having to hold her arms out through five verses of a carol! The angel always wore a white robe with tinsel around the edge of the wings and a tinsel halo on her head.

The Sunday school teachers put gifts under the tree for their class members, and the children couldn't wait for their names to be called. Even the mothers got a little anxious at times—Ruby Doggett didn't think that they were ever going to call her son Clark's name one year when he was small. She sat there praying that he wouldn't be overlooked—and he wasn't.

I think both churches provided "treats" for all who came to the program. The treats were always in small brown paper bags (maybe white paper bags were used in later years). The treats probably differed from year to year, but usually they contained an apple, an orange, a tangerine, a pack of chewing gum, some hard candy (or, in later years, a candy bar), a few nuts in the shells and raisins. I'm not sure but I think that the raisins many years ago were still attached to the stems that they grew on. Margaret Metz said that her father, John Medearis, and other storeowners in Summerfield used to order boxes of hard candy for the churches to put in the treat bags.

The carols, the trees, the programs and the treat bags put joy in the hearts and stars in the eyes of the children at Christmas.

CAR CHASE TURNED HOUSE UPSIDE DOWN

Miss Mittie Jackson, who taught at the old two-story school in Summerfield, boarded for a few years with the John Medearis family. She said there was never a dull moment at their home. That was certainly true of a night in 1925.

Two Greensboro teachers, a Greensboro attorney and another man were driving back to Greensboro one night, heading south toward Summerfield. Suddenly, as they neared the Rockingham County line about 11:00 p.m., a car started chasing them.

The foursome assumed that the car was carrying robbers and sped up to try to outrun them. They managed to stay ahead of the car until they got to Summerfield. There the car got in front of them just as they neared the Medearis house.

It was the middle of the night, and Mr. and Mrs. Medearis had probably been asleep for several hours in their bedroom. Suddenly running feet, breaking glass and screams shattered the silence of the night. The two women had jumped from the car, run up on the front porch of the Medearis house and jumped through the closed window, breaking the sash and the windowpanes. They ran into the bedroom shouting that murderers were after them. What a rude awakening for the Medearis family!

Mr. Medearis leaped from the bed and began searching for his pistol. By the time he got to the front window, he found the men who'd been with the teachers trying to get in. He knocked one of them back onto the

The John F. Medearis House, where the car chase ended. *Courtesy Bill Gordon.*

front porch. The men tried to tell him that they were with the girls and that highwaymen were after them.

Just then, the two officers who had been chasing the foursome arrived. Mr. Medearis, who was a magistrate at the time, recognized one of the men as a federal prohibition officer. The officers explained that they had been warned to be on the lookout for a car carrying whiskey, and they thought the car they had been pursuing was the culprit.

In the meantime, one of the teachers had locked herself in a closet, and the other one hid in a corner of one of the rooms. Mrs. Medearis, afraid for her life, was finally found in a back room, with the barrel of a gun poking through the crack of the door. In his hurry to find his pistol, Mr. Medearis had torn his nightshirt on a nail. One of the teachers had fainted, and no doubt they were all quaking in their boots.

The officers apologized for frightening everyone, and the attorney agreed to pay for the damage to the window if the officers wouldn't do so. It's not known if the neighbors heard the commotion, but after so much excitement, there was probably no more sleep at the Medearis house that night.

Is that a Firecracker, or Did Bank Robbers Strike Again?

The young man who entered the Bank of Summerfield about 10:15 a.m. one morning in May 1922 was neatly dressed in a dark, pinstripe suit but wasn't wearing a collar. He pulled his pistol and ordered Howard Simpson and B.H. "Ben" Hoskins to put up their hands. The robber apparently judged them too slow at following orders and snarled, "I mean business."

He then forced the two men to enter the vault and tried to lock them in, but Simpson had turned the combination on the door so that it couldn't be locked. The robber then marched them outside, grabbing about $1,500 from the cash drawer on the way out. Still waving his pistol, he ran across an open field, with Simpson and others running after him. When the robber reached a patch of pinewoods, his pursuers lost him.

Simpson, according to historian Margaret Metz, was the teller, cashier, bookkeeper and janitor. Mr. Hoskins was one of the bank directors. Hoskins later remarked that, since the bank was protected by insurance, he thought he'd rather collect bank insurance than for his family to collect life insurance.

This was not the first attempt to rob the bank. Just three months earlier, less than two years after the bank opened in July 1920, thieves struck during the night. They battered their way through the door of the vault but were unable to open the safe door. They had taken tools from the railroad section house nearby, but the crowbars, sledgehammer, chisel and pick were not enough to get into the safe. All they got for their trouble was fifteen cents and a box of cigars.

Inside the Bank of Summerfield, where the bank robberies took place. Guy Brittain Sr. is looking through the teller window, while the others are unknown. *Courtesy Bob Brittain.*

Three years after the second robbery, the bank was robbed for the third time in 1925, this time by three young men. Within fifteen minutes of the robbery, all three were captured. Two of the young men had entered the bank and asked for change. But instead of pulling a bill from his pocket, one of them pulled a small revolver. Then he cracked the cashier on the head with the gun. When Howard Simpson sank to the floor, they took all the cash in sight and walked boldly out the front door to a waiting car.

The three young men drove off toward Greensboro, but the alarm had been spread. The men of the village quickly armed themselves and gave chase. About twenty yards down the road, the driver was so scared or excited that he drove the car into a post, to the disgust of the other two boys. The boys jumped out of the car and ran; that's when people might have wondered if someone was shooting off firecrackers. But it wasn't firecrackers; it was the start of a gun battle—in the quiet little village of Summerfield!

After learning that the bank had been robbed and taking time to grab their guns, some of the men caught up with the would-be bank robbers. V.W. Wagoner, armed with a shotgun, ran the boys out into the open. Ben Calhoun, a deaf mute, captured one of the boys after shooting the dust from under his feet. Finally, all the boys were surrounded and they surrendered.

Fortunately, no one was injured in the gun battle, and all but twenty dollars of the stolen money was recovered. Part of the money was found on one of the robbers, and part of it had been hidden by one of the robbers in a gully while they were trying to outrun the local men. Ralph Robinson remembered that Max Robinson, his brother, who was just a young boy at the time, found the money in the gully and turned it in. Maybe all the excitement was what caused Max to decide to become a Greensboro policeman when he grew up.

Summerfield's Long-Ago NASCAR Connection

A few people from Summerfield got into racing during the early years of NASCAR. They got in on the ground floor, so to speak; all of their racing was done on dirt tracks. But before that, there were motorcycle races on Hamburg Mill Road in the late 1930s.

A motorcycle club in Greensboro leased the land and built a track. It was about three-tenths of a mile long and had a one-strand wire fence around the track. There were usually twenty-five or thirty people racing at a time. The winner would get a tire or a shoe; the left shoe had a steel bottom so they could drag their foot in the turns. The track was on Glenn Brown's property.

Herbert Scarlette remembered going, as a small boy, with his dad, and Odell Brown remembers climbing a tree to watch the races. The races probably stopped shortly after the beginning of World War II.

Some of the race car owners were Herbert Scarlette, Bill Wall, Donald Price, Byrd Johnson, Jimmy Mabe, Bill Pegram, Jack Hedrick, Fred Perdue, Andrew Winfree and Gene Bull. One of Bob Welborn's cars was owned jointly with R.W. Winfree, Junior Jones and Dewey Trogdon Jr. Using part of his mustering-out pay from the navy in 1953, Dewey bought a radiator and a set of tires to become a part owner.

Some of the drivers were Bill Pegram, Walter Flinchum, Donald Tucker, Andrew Winfree, Jack Hedrick and Bob Welborn. Bob won the 1957 convertible championship with a '57 Chevy. Jack Hedrick didn't start driving until after Bill Pegram quit. When Andrew Winfree was racing at Dover Downs, he had a wreck; the ignition switch was on the left side of the dash and it was embedded in his kneecap.

During the 1950s and 1960s, they raced at Bowman-Gray Stadium in Winston-Salem; Ace Speedway at Altamahaw; the fairgrounds at Greensboro; Blair Park at High Point; at tracks at Hickory, Charlotte and North Wilkesboro; Caraway at Asheboro; Horse Pasture, Virginia; Martinsville, Virginia; and possibly others, which were all NASCAR tracks. They also raced at Diamond Speedway at Stokesdale and 311 Racetrack at Madison, but those were not NASCAR tracks.

At times, the cars were almost a community effort. People were on the lookout for a junk car in somebody's yard where they'd pick up a car body for ten or fifteen dollars. Sometimes, they could get a car body at Summerfield Auto Parts. Occasionally, they got a free motor when the Ford or Chevrolet dealer in Greensboro was going to discard an old one. After they got the bodies and motors, they did a lot of work on both to get them ready to race.

At first, they worked on the cars at "Syke" Scarlette's garage and then at Herbert Scarlette's garage on Scalesville Road. They souped up the motors and put roll bars in the cars. When she was about twelve years old, Herbert Scarlette's daughter, Nina, helped by putting lifters in a Chevrolet motor. If they were working on a car and needed more parts, some of the men who were standing around watching and talking would say, "Here's a few dollars, go buy the parts." George Price did a lot of welding on the cars. Some of the cars were worked on at Lindsay Parrish's garage on U.S. 220, near Strawberry Road.

At times the cars advertised for Guilford Tobacco Warehouse. They put a number and the driver's name on the car. The drivers wore football helmets, and the doors were tied together with a leather strap. Sometimes they tested the cars by driving them around the lake behind the school.

Since the tracks were dirt, there was a lot of dust. Even though they put water and calcium on the track, people still got covered in dust even if they were just watching. It only cost two or three dollars to watch the races. There were programs with pictures of the drivers. The drivers would even get out and help change tires. They had a five-gallon can of extra gas at the pit stop, which they hardly ever used.

Car driven in NASCAR races by Jack Hedrick. It was built by Gene Bull, Jack Hedrick, Fred Perdue and Tommy Hedrick. *Courtesy Jack Hedrick.*

The first race was only ten laps, and the fastest cars qualified to run in the forty-lap race. Sometimes, other car owners would loan the driver a tire or a part so they could finish the race. When the cars were hauled on Bill Wall's truck, the only way to unload the car was to back the truck up to a dirt bank and drive the car off.

In the late 1960s, Jack Hedrick, Fred Perdue and Gene Bull owned the car in the photo. Jack drove the car and held the track record for several years at 311 Speedway at Madison and Caraway at Asheboro. They won several races; at that time first prize was $500, and that was big money!

IN THE PAST, CHRISTMAS BROUGHT SIMPLE JOYS

My aunt Clara Angel, at ninety-four years of age, remembered celebrating Christmas when she was a child. She grew up on a farm and money was scarce. Her father was a tenant farmer and raised tobacco. They grew most of their food and didn't go to the store for many things.

Every year, before Christmas, Grandma (Clara's mother) made molasses taffy. She used molasses that Grandpa had made. She boiled sugar and molasses and after it was cooked and was cool enough to handle, Grandma and Myrtle, the oldest girl, pulled the taffy and cut it into small pieces. Aunt Clara said that all the children really looked forward to the molasses taffy because that was a rare treat.

Grandpa always went hunting and shot a wild turkey for Christmas dinner. Along with the turkey, they had canned green beans, stewed Irish potatoes and baked sweet potatoes. Grandma didn't make dressing to go with the turkey. Instead, she fixed pea-cakes. She boiled black-eyed peas or crowder peas and mixed them with cornbread crumbs, sage, salt and pepper. After she mixed all this, she'd take some of the mixture, roll it into balls and flatten it out into patties. After she got all the mixture made into patties, she put all the pea-cakes in a pan and baked them in the oven. They were probably almost as good as the dressing we have now and probably tasted about the same.

They usually had a fresh coconut cake for dessert at Christmas; that was Grandma's favorite cake. When she cracked the coconut shell and got all the coconut out, she used half of the shell to keep salt in. When she got ready to cook a meal, she'd get out the coconut shell of salt, and as soon as she was finished, the shell filled with salt went right back into the cupboard. Salt had to be bought at the store, so it was used with care.

They didn't have a Christmas tree, so they put out their shoes so Santa Claus would know where to leave their things. Sometimes they left their shoes in front of the fireplace and sometimes at the foot of the bed. Each child usually got a stick of peppermint candy and some mittens or stockings that Grandma had knitted. When Aunt Clara was about six or seven years old, she got a small china doll from Santa. She was the youngest child, and that was the last time Santa Claus came to see them.

Grandma had told them that Santa would come down the chimney. When they lived at the Clay Brittain farm, there was a big fireplace in the kitchen. On Christmas morning, the children would run and look to see if Santa had loosened any soot when he came down the chimney. Sure enough, with the help of Grandma or Grandpa, there was always a little soot on the hearth.

When I was growing up, we didn't put out our shoes for Santa; we put out shoeboxes! We did have a Christmas tree, but it always had to be a cedar tree. Daddy usually went out and chopped down a tree for us.

Sometimes we'd tell him that we'd like to have a pine tree, but he always came back with a cedar.

We didn't go to the store to talk to Santa Claus like children do now. If anybody came to visit, the grown-ups would always ask children what they wanted Santa to bring them. We always ended our list, which was short, with nuts, fruits and candy. Even when children wrote letters to Santa and they were printed in the newspaper, they all asked for nuts, fruits and candy. I suppose that was because we didn't get many of those things all during the year.

We were told that Santa Claus brought our toys but that your parents had to pay Santa for them so we didn't ask for a lot of things. There was no TV to see all the new toys, only the Sears catalogue or "wish book." Sears always put out a special Christmas catalogue, which was smaller than the regular catalogue. It had clothes and other things, but what the children were interested in were the toys! They had pages and pages of dolls, wagons and other toys to tempt the children. Times were simpler then and we didn't have many things, but we were happy with our few toys and our nuts, fruits and candy.

FUNERAL TRADITIONS CHANGED OVER TIME

Funeral customs were quite different when I was growing up. One of the first things that was done when a family member died was to stop the clock—at least that was the custom in some families. There were no battery or electric clocks then. The clocks had to be wound, some of them once a day and some of them about once a week. The clock wouldn't be started up again until after the funeral.

In earlier years, the body was not embalmed. Neighbors washed and dressed the body. Later, when embalming became more prevalent, the body was carried to the funeral home for embalming but was returned to the family's home until time for the funeral. Most people used Vaughn's Funeral Home in Stokesdale after it was opened in 1930. Friends or family members sat up during the night at the home of the deceased. I remember sitting up all night once; it was the longest night I'd ever experienced! There was coffee to drink and food to nibble on, but it was still almost impossible to stay awake.

It was probably during the 1950s before the visitation was held at the funeral home, at least in the Summerfield area. Some home visitation continued until the early 1960s. Friends and neighbors carried food for the family of the deceased, and before paper plates, plastic and foil were available, all of the food was in dishes or pans that had to be returned to the people who had prepared the food. That could take several days because you always wanted to stay and visit for a while when you returned the dishes.

If a family lived in an area in which there were lots of close neighbors, someone always went around the neighborhood and collected for a floral wreath from "the Neighbors." At most funerals, there were flower girls; they could be family members such as nieces or grandchildren. Sometimes Sunday school class members served as flower girls. They sat in a group at the church and carried the flowers to the cemetery at the close of the funeral. At times, the flower girls carried the flowers from the house to the vehicle used to take the flowers to the church. I remember thinking that I'd be glad when I was old enough to be a flower girl.

Back then, all the women and older girls wore hats and gloves to church and to funerals. Most people dressed in black or dark colors for funerals. I remember once when one of our aunts arrived at a funeral wearing a brightly flowered dress. The whole family was horrified!

For years all the graves were dug by hand using picks and shovels. There was a group of men from each church who usually took care of the digging. Some of the men who dug graves at the Baptist church were Alfred Parrish, Jasper Angel, Cephas and Jesse Shelton, Earle Trogdon, Arthur Ellington and Fred Michaux. Some of the men who dug graves at the Methodist church were Bob Wright, Lee Tilley, William Gamble, Alton Sharon and Harold Decker. At Peace Church, Jim Burkes and his son Charlie helped to dig graves. Charlie said it wasn't too hard unless you ran into rock while you were digging. I'm sure there were others besides these. They never charged for this service; it was just a show of respect for the family. An infant's grave dug by Sammy Angel in 1997 was probably the last hand-dug grave in the Summerfield area.

At least one man in Summerfield made caskets for people in the community. Margaret Medearis Metz said that her grandfather, G.J. Smith (1824–1902), was the casket-maker for many years. In Stokesdale in 1887, H.L. Gant made coffins, as well as coaches and buggies. Some families probably made pine boxes for their own family members, and in earlier times the casket was often carried to the church on a horse-drawn wagon.

The Summerfield Quartet, which was composed of Clyde Pegram, (Mr.) Della Clayton, Dalton Davis and John Smith, sang at many funerals in the Summerfield area. T.D. Alley sang in the quartet after John Smith died. They also sang at many church services and at homecomings. Mrs. Lillian Davis accompanied the quartet.

One funeral made a lasting impression on my oldest sister, Lucille Angel Pope. Jane Roach, a great-aunt, died in 1929; she was a very heavy woman. Since she lived across the road from Summerfield Methodist Church, where the funeral was held, they didn't use a wagon or a hearse. When they started carrying the coffin, probably a pine box, to the church, the bottom of the coffin seemed about to fall out! They had to stop and nail some more boards onto the coffin before they could proceed to the church and have the funeral.

IN WARTIME, CARPOOLING WAS SIMPLY A WAY OF LIFE

Getting to work in Greensboro and back home at the end of the day could be quite a challenge during World War II and for several years after. Those of us just starting in the workforce didn't have a car, and most people were lucky to have one car for the whole family. We carpooled even though we'd never heard of the word.

People had to be innovative to solve the problem. I remember riding with my brother, Marvin Angel, to the Sears Mail Order Plant on Lawndale Drive in the mornings, along with Hilda Scarlette, Virginia Everette and several others. Then we rode the city bus on downtown to work at Jefferson Life Insurance Company. In the afternoon, we rode home with someone else or rode the "Blue Goose."

After the Gate City Transit Line started a bus service from Greensboro to Summerfield, Oak Ridge and Stokesdale, lots of people rode the bus home. Everybody called it the "Blue Goose," and you got a long ride for your money. It went out Lake Brandt Road to get to Summerfield instead of going out Highway 220. Ivery Hutchins was one of the bus drivers.

In 1944, the fare was thirty cents to Oak Ridge and forty cents to Stokesdale. It must have been twenty or twenty-five cents to Summerfield. When Virginia Everette, my sister Hilda and I were all working at

Paul Murphy's 1941 Plymouth and riders. *Standing, left to right*: Mattie Belle Winfree, Edith Proctor, possibly Helen Jones, Guy Ayers, Max Gardner and Zeb Case. *Inside the car*: Paul, George E. "Jack" Winfree, William "Bill" Wall and Clyde Robinson Jr. *Courtesy Barbara Angel Cockman.*

Jefferson, we would stop at a little grocery store in the 100 block of East Market Street. We'd get a snack on our way to catch the "Blue Goose" on Davie Street after work. One of our favorite snacks was a five-cent dill pickle and a ten-cent package of crackers.

Most everybody who had a car carried riders to Greensboro. Some of them were Marion Ayers, Elizabeth Ogburn, Marie Burchett, Charlie Gardner, Troy Stantliff Sr., Guy Ayers and Ralph Vaughn. I also remember riding with Marion Johnson and Addie Winfree. There were probably lots of other drivers who carried riders.

During World War II, gas and tires for cars were in short supply. Paul Murphy drove to Mock-Judson and packed as many people in the car as he could. Sometimes two of the boys would even ride in the trunk! Alma Tilley remembers that Troy Stantliff worked at a poultry company on Davie Street. He drove there and got out, and Alma drove his car to drop the other riders off at the Blue Bell plant on South Elm Street. Then she drove on to the Blue Bell plant on East Lee Street, where she worked. After work, she parked the car near the poultry company, and she and the other riders would shop at the Kress and Woolworth stores while they waited for Troy to finish work. Alma said that Troy kept a little stool in his car between the front and back seats, and one of the riders sat on the stool. How many people would do that now to get to their jobs?

One time there was an ice storm while we were at work. The streets were slick, and I don't think the city buses were running. Someone told us that if you put socks on over your shoes, you wouldn't slide on the ice as much. So Hilda and I bought socks, probably at the Woolworth or Kress store, and proceeded to walk to the apartment of our sister and brother-in-law, Ila and Macon Ingold, on Asheboro Street. It was down past Asheboro Street Baptist Church, which was a long, long walk. Evidently the socks worked since neither of us fell. I don't remember if we had to walk back to the Jefferson Building the next morning; maybe the city buses were running then. Now people complain if they have to walk a block!

When we finally did get a car, finding a parking place was the challenge. Some people parked ten or twelve blocks away, where parking on the street was free. There were no parking garages uptown, but there were parking lots where you could park and pay by the month. I remember parking at a service station several blocks beyond the Masonic Temple, which was about six or seven blocks away.

Working in the Jefferson Building had its advantages; we'd hang out the windows on the sixteenth floor and over the balcony railing on the seventeenth floor to watch the Christmas parades. The A&T Band and the Shriners' Band always did something special at Jefferson Square, and we had a birds-eye view.

We also had access to all the stores downtown and knew where we wanted to spend our next paycheck before we got it. The Woolworth and Kress stores both had a lunch counter, and the Minute Sandwich Shop was on Market Street. There was also a sandwich shop in the Southeastern Building, and some of the drugstores had a soda fountain. We enjoyed going to Meyer's Department Store to get vegetable soup and cornbread and to the Lotus for Chinese food. There were the S&W and Mayfair Cafeterias, and Yelverton's Barbecue was on Greene Street, so we had a good choice of places to eat lunch. We didn't make much money, and even though it was a challenge to get to work and back, we were glad to have jobs, made lots of friends and stored up many memories.

An Unusual Wedding in 1937

They got married where? When Ruby Morton and Robert Williams got married in 1937 at the Carolina Theatre in Greensboro, it must have been big news in the Summerfield area.

My oldest sister, Lucille Angel Pope, included in her diary, "Iver [Angel], Lib [Winfree], Earlene [Parrish], Lee [Scarlette] and me went to see Robert Williams and Ruby Morton get married at the Carolina Theater." The entry was dated November 19, 1937, and when I read it recently it aroused my curiosity. I contacted Ruby's nephew Robert Morton and his wife Billie Lou to get information about the wedding. They remembered seeing a picture and hearing about the wedding. With their help, I got in touch with other family members.

The newspaper announcement stated that the marriage took place at the Carolina Theatre. The Reverend B.C. Reavis of College Place Methodist Church officiated. Gladys Morton, sister of the bride, was the maid of honor. Bridesmaids were Margaret Morton, sister of the bride; Marie Rayle; Mrs. William Scott; and Mrs. Lorraine Daniels. Peggy Miles was the flower girl.

Pat Kasey was the best man, and ushers were Roscoe Tuttle, Lloyd Pugh, Bill Williams and J.C. Davis. Ruby's father, Geter B. Morton, wore a tux for the first time and walked his daughter down the aisle—over his very strong objections. Ruby told him he *had* to do it. A men's clothing store in Greensboro loaned the tuxedos for the men in the wedding party, remembers Otilla Morton Cummings, another sister.

Otilla thinks that Lerner's Dress Shop might have loaned the dresses for the bride, the maid of honor and the bridesmaids. Otilla made the dress for the flower girl. She also remembers that a Greensboro florist furnished the flowers for the wedding, free of charge, but doesn't remember which florist. Ruby's wedding ring was donated by Schiffman's Jewelers in Greensboro.

Robert Williams and Hugh Morton, who was the manager of the theatre at the time, had been in the navy together, and that's how it came about that the wedding took place there, Otilla remembers. She doesn't remember the music but does remember that the theatre was filled. No announcements were sent out so everybody who knew the couple was welcome to attend.

Their brief honeymoon of one night was spent in the bridal suite of the O'Henry Hotel, compliments of the hotel. Otilla remembers that

Bride and attendants at Carolina Theatre in 1937. *Left to right*: Mrs. Lorraine Daniels, Margaret Morton, Ruby Morton Williams, Norma Scott, Marie Rayle and Gladys Morton. The flower girl is Peggy Miles. *Courtesy Woodley Williams.*

their immediate family went with the couple to the hotel room and stayed a short time. She thinks that the flowers in the room were furnished by the hotel. She also thinks the hotel furnished breakfast for the couple the next morning.

Woodley Williams, the couple's son, remembers his mother mentioning a fur jacket or stole, and Otilla said that it was donated to the bride by Jones Furriers. A furniture company, maybe Burtner's, gave the couple a stove and refrigerator. Morrison-Neese Furniture Company gave them a bedroom suite, and another store gave them a set of dishes.

Shortly after the wedding, Ruby was honored with a kitchen shower by family and friends—so the couple was well-prepared to set up housekeeping near Summerfield. Unfortunately, after their storybook wedding, the couple's happy marriage was cut short when Robert died in 1954. Family members still like to reminisce about the unusual wedding.

Easter Egg Hunts and Sunrise Services

Back in the 1940s and 1950s, there were no plastic Easter eggs. Many people in Summerfield just went to the chicken house to get eggs to dye. You hoped that there wouldn't be any hens in the nests to peck your hands when you reached for the eggs! Then you boiled the eggs and, last of all, dyed them.

Sometimes dyeing the eggs was a challenge when you couldn't go to the store and buy the dyeing kits. Dewey Trogdon remembers his mother using beet juice to dye eggs; she saved some of the beet juice when she canned beet pickles. Their chickens laid brown eggs, so the color wasn't as pretty as they would have been with white eggs. Rachel Terrell said that her mother dyed eggs for them and thinks that they might have colored some of the eggs with crayons. They didn't have Easter baskets and carried the eggs in paper bags to the egg hunts.

Bill Gordon remembers helping his mother dye eggs; they used tablets that you dissolved in hot water and then dipped the eggs. They hid the eggs at home and at their grandparents' home; he doesn't remember any egg hunts at church. One of Linda Ayers Southard's early memories was an egg hunt at the old Methodist parsonage. The eggs were hidden in the woods near the parsonage; this was before Linda started to school.

The Sunday school teachers weren't too pleased when Gene Barham peeled and ate some of the eggs before the egg hunt was over! He doesn't remember any prizes, but they had cookies and Kool-Aid for refreshments. Dewey Trogdon also remembers being more interested in eating the eggs than hunting for them.

When her grandfather, "Sheriff Joe" Hoskins, was still living, Elizabeth Hoskins remembers going to his house to hunt eggs. The eggs were already dyed and hidden when the children arrived. "Aunt Emma," not related but thought of as an aunt, Aunt Nelle and Aunt Kate Hoskins dyed and hid the eggs.

Hattaway's Seed Store and Woolworth in Greensboro sold dyed baby chicks, or biddies, at Easter for several years. The chicks were dyed different pastel colors, and the children loved them. Mildred and Tommy Pope and David Angel received dyed biddies, but the biddies didn't live long. Margaret Chandler said that she and John got one for their children Maurice and Donna one year, but when the children fussed a bit over the biddy, they wouldn't buy them anymore.

Ready for an Easter egg hunt about 1953 at the home of Mr. and Mrs. W.A. Scarlette, Grandma and Pa to the children. *Left to right*: Mildred Pope, Carolyn Nelson (almost hidden), Jean Angel, Michael Ingold, Donald Nelson, Barbara Angel, Dwight Angel (almost hidden), Judy Angel and Tommy Pope. *Courtesy the author.*

Margaret Wilson remembers that she and her brother and sisters got a new basket every year. The baskets contained dyed eggs, a chocolate rabbit and other candy, as well as a stuffed bunny sometimes.

Little girls, as well as older ones, looked forward to new dresses at Easter. Jean Angel Stofanik remembers that she and her sister, Judy, usually got new summer shoes at Easter, too. Mildred Pope Jessup remembers that one of her Easter dresses was made from a feed sack. She also got an Easter bonnet, or hat, that probably came from Woolworth. When she got black patent shoes and a little pocketbook one year, she thought she was ready to *lead* the Easter parade.

Bea Stafford Curtis remembers having an egg hunt for her class when she was teaching at Summerfield School one year. They hid the eggs along the chicken lot fence—on the outside, of course. For several years, the Summerfield Fire Department has held egg hunts for all the children of the community.

At our house, some of the adults would play games with the children on one side of the house while other adults hid the eggs on another side of the house. Sometimes the dog found some of the eggs before the children got to them.

With all the fun of new dresses, dyed eggs, baskets and egg hunts, the real meaning of Easter was not overlooked. Summerfield Methodist Church has had sunrise services since the 1950s, Louise Styers remembers. One year it snowed and they still had the service outside. Peace Church has had sunrise services for many years but not always every year, and the same was true of the egg hunts.

The first sunrise service at the Baptist church might have been in 1964. Sometimes it was held on the lawn in front of the Education Building, and the choir stood on the steps. It seemed that it always got cold before Easter, and some of the teenage girls would stand outside in their thin dresses with no coat on so everybody could see their new Easter dresses. I don't know how they kept from freezing! It's been several years since the Baptist church has had a sunrise service.

Moravia Moravian Church, as far back as Rachel Terrell can remember, has had a sunrise service on Easter Sunday. In earlier years, the band would go to the homes of the sick and elderly members and play for them before the sunrise service was held.

The week before Easter, the congregation still scrubs the tombstones in the cemetery. At times, some of the Sunday school classes wanted to raise money for projects and would scrub the stones for a small fee.

Many years ago, the Moravians had a sit-down breakfast before the sunrise service, but in recent years they changed to having ham and sausage biscuits after the service. The service starts in the sanctuary, and then everybody walks out to the cemetery. The choir sings and the band plays; they always try to be in the cemetery when the sun rises. Rachel remembers very few times when rain kept them from going outside. Watching the sunrise and thinking about the first Easter gives you a really special feeling.

It's Time to Churn

Years ago, we always had a cow, and the only name I remember each one being called was Bossy. Daddy and the boys always did the milking. Mama and Lucille, my oldest sister, could milk, but I guess it was considered a man's job. Most of us younger girls never learned how to milk. Looking after the milk was definitely women's work.

When it was time to milk the cow, all the cats gathered around in the stable hoping that the milker would squirt some milk into their mouths. The milk was always good, except when the wild onions came up in the spring; if the cow ate a lot of wild onions, you could hardly drink the milk. Fortunately that didn't last long.

The milk had to be strained through a cloth and poured into gallon-sized glass jars and stored in the icebox or the refrigerator after we had electricity. I think the jars came from the school cafeteria; they must have purchased mayonnaise and mustard in gallon jars.

Before people had iceboxes, they had various ways of keeping milk, butter and other food from spoiling. Bill Cummings remembers that the Travis Sharon family had a cement box or trough in the branch near the spring. The water flowed through holes or openings in the box to keep the food cool. Others put food in the well bucket and let the bucket down just far enough in the water to keep the food cool.

My aunt, Clara Angel, said that they had a milk hole when they lived at the Clay Brittain farm. Grandpa dug a hole about the size of a grave near the house and even built steps to go down into it. He put boards in the bottom to set the food on and then made a cover of boards to keep animals out. Necessity really was the mother of invention for folks in earlier times.

We had plenty of milk and cream for whipped cream—the real thing, not the kind of topping you get in a container at the grocery store now. We used to come home from school and fix hot chocolate. We'd skim off enough cream from the top of the milk to have whipped cream in our cocoa. How good that was.

The way we enjoyed whipped cream the most was with Mama's strawberry stack pies in the spring. We usually had a small strawberry patch or picked some at a neighbor's patch. Mama would bake several pie crusts; there were no frozen ones back then. After the berries were washed, chopped and sweetened, she'd put a browned crust in a large plate, fill it with strawberries, stack another crust and fill it with berries and keep on like this until all the crusts were used. Then came the whipped cream on top. That was really good eating!

There was always enough milk to let some of it "turn" or clabber, and then it was time to churn. We had an ironstone churn with a wooden dasher. The lid to the churn had a hole in the middle for the dasher handle, and you sat and lifted the dasher up and down until the butter formed. Your arm would get so tired you thought it would fall off.

Jar rack or jar tree made from a cedar tree.
Courtesy Irene Clodfelter.

Later we had a square metal churn with removable wooden lids; the churn sat inside a metal frame. That one had a wheel on the frame that you turned around and around until the butter formed. It was a little easier on the arm than the dasher churn.

My grandmother Elizabeth Josephine Scarlette (1878–1950) taught her small daughters, Dianna and Clara, a short rhyme to recite while they were churning. They probably used a dasher churn. The rhyme was: "Come, butter come; Peter's standing at the gate; Waiting for a butter cake; Come, butter come." I wonder how many times they repeated it while they were churning.

After the butter formed, you dipped the butter out into a large pan and poured the buttermilk from the churn into jars. The buttermilk would have little flecks of butter in it and was delicious, especially with corn bread crumbled into a glass full of buttermilk.

The next step was to work, or knead, all the milk from the butter—another workout for your arm. Then it was time to mold the butter. The molds were made of wood, and ours had a sheaf of wheat carved into the mold. The butter was packed tightly into the mold, with no air holes, and the sheaf of wheat design showed up on the top of the butter after it was taken out of the mold. I think ours was a half-pound mold. Sometimes Mama would sell some butter to a neighbor, but we ate a lot of it with her good hot biscuits. We always had plenty of butter to put in vegetables when they were cooked, and a special treat was apples sliced and fried in butter.

After the butter and buttermilk were taken care of, all of the jars and the churn had to be washed and scalded. Then the jars were hung outside on the jar rack, or jar tree, in the sun and fresh air so there was no milk smell. Of course, when the jars needed to be used again they had to be rewashed after you shook out any little spiders that had taken up residence inside the jars.

The jar rack was similar to what is now called a bottle tree, but the jar rack was actually a cedar tree that had been cut down and put into the ground like a post. Cedars had a lot of small limbs that were cut off but left long enough to hang the jars on. There was a lot of work involved from the time the cow was milked until you finished up—but that whipped cream, buttermilk and fresh-churned butter was worth all the work.

SUMMERFIELD RESIDENTS DEVOTED TO SERVICE

Although Summerfield was just a small community, the people worked together for the Red Cross. The Greensboro chapter of the American Red Cross was organized on April 11, 1917, with fourteen charter members. About five months later, the Summerfield Auxiliary was organized on September 19, 1917, with a membership of twenty. The Greensboro chapter minutes for September 28, 1917, reported twenty-seven members. The Stokesdale branch or auxiliary was organized on May 15, 1918, and the Oak Ridge auxiliary was organized on July 10, 1918.

Thanks to Ellen Metz von Nardroff, a small notebook containing some of the minutes and names of members had been saved, a very important part of our history. The organizational meeting took place at the home of Miss Nell Hoskins, but the next meeting was held at the two-story post office, which was located near the depot. The new auxiliary got right to work making bed shirts and knitting garments.

A committee was appointed to get names and addresses of enlisted men from the Summerfield area in order to send Thanksgiving boxes to them. The minutes didn't state what the boxes would contain.

Some of the men from the Summerfield area who served in World War I were Benjamin H. Angel, Dwight Brittain, Robert Byrd, Stacy Calhoun, Jesse and John H. Carter, Thaddeus J. Clayton, Cleo and Zeb Archie Davis, Thomas Doggett, Wade A. Durham, Robert Gamble, Martin Luther Hall, John Holbrook, Bob and C.W. Horsford, Holly and Nicholas Johnson, Zeb V. Jones, Jasper A. Ladd, Herman Linville, Thomas Lloyd, Joseph A. Long, Hugh Victor Martin, Dr. Herbert Ogburn, Bryan H. Parrish,

John Roberson, Fred and Henry Clay Smith, John Henry Soyars, John L. Stanley, Floyd Stigall, Joseph Thorpe, Charles W. Vernon, Richard Waynick, Clay Moore Wilson, Dr. N.G. Wilson and Raymond W. Winfree. There were probably others from the area also.

In March 1918, it was reported that twelve comfort pillows had been finished, forty-three knitted garments had been completed and turned in and eighteen pairs of pajamas had been made and sent in to the Red Cross. The group decided to make twelve additional comfort pillows. For several months the auxiliary met upstairs above the post office, but then the meeting place was changed to the school building.

Sometime before September 1, the Summerfield group furnished the following to the Greensboro Chapter Canteen to be distributed to troops en route: ten bushels of fruit, seven fried chickens, six dozen eggs, ten loaves of bread, six dozen cakes, one hundred apple pies, pickles, several jars of jelly, pears, grapes, peaches and watermelons. Surely the one hundred pies must have been small fried apple pies. The group had also completed twenty-four pajama suits and twenty-four operating gowns.

The December 24, 1917 edition of the *Greensboro Patriot* reported that the Summerfield Auxiliary had sixty members, but they were not stopping with that. The paper complimented the group on the number of beautifully made garments and knitted articles that had been turned in. The concluding statement noted that "if every community in Guilford would do as well there would be no room to charge indifference and lack of patriotism on the part of country people."

A partial listing of wartime committees gives an interesting picture of activities in Greensboro through the Red Cross during this period. On September 28, 1917, Miss Katherine Hoskins of Summerfield was appointed to collect data for a history of Guilford County Women in the World War.

Contained in the notebook of minutes was a letter from Hugh Wilson, a young man from Summerfield, to the local auxiliary complimenting the group for their work and telling them how much the soldiers in France appreciated the Red Cross. He was working at Camp Hospital 26 in November 1918 and knew the situation firsthand.

At one time, the local auxiliary membership reached 176. In January 1919, twenty-four refugee shirts had been made and returned. That was the last notation, and it is unknown when the auxiliary was disbanded or discontinued.

Bryan H. Parrish was one of the men from Summerfield who served in the army during World War I. *Courtesy the author.*

At the present time, at least one Summerfield resident devotes a lot of time to Red Cross work. Earline Huffman works most Tuesday afternoons and Saturday mornings at the Greensboro Red Cross. Community Lutheran, Summerfield Methodist, Center Methodist and First Baptist Churches of Summerfield take turns hosting the blood drives in the Summerfield area. So, for almost one hundred years, the people of Summerfield have been doing their part for the American Red Cross.